Kaleidoscope

2 Reading and Writing

Anita Sökmen
University of Washington

Daphne Mackey
University of Washington

HOUGHTON MIFFLIN COMPANY   Boston   New York

Sponsoring Editor: Susan Maguire
Senior Associate Editor: Kathleen Sands Boehmer
Associate Project Editor: Gabrielle Stone
Senior Production/Design Coordinator: Carol Merrigan
Senior Manufacturing Coordinator: Marie Barnes
Marketing Manager: Elaine Leary

Cover Design: Ha Nguyen
Cover Image: Hiser, David. Mexico, Publa, 'Quetzal Dancers' Dressed in Aztec style costumes, ©Tony Stone worldwide.

Pages 66–67: Roger E. Axtell, "Gestures: The Do's and Taboos of Body Language Around the World," pp. 9, 43. Copyright © 1991 by Roger E. Axtell. Reprinted by permission of John Wiley & Sons, Inc.
Pages 83–84: From *Parade*, December 29, 1996. Copyright © 1996. Used by permission of *Parade* and the *Lexington Herald-Leader*.
Pages 89–90: Adapted with permission from "The Healing Power of Pets" by Walter J. Cheney. Copyright © 1996, The Writers' Consortium, http://www.seniors-site.com.
Page 112: From "Why Do Cats Sulk?" by Arline Bleecker (Boca Raton: Globe Communications, 1996), p. 91. Adapted by permission of the publisher.
Page 117: Adapted from "Keeping Fit: Walks of Life" by Simon Chaitowitz, *Northwest Health*, March/April 1997, pp. 8–9. Reprinted by permission of the author. Source: American Podiatric Medical Association.
Page 120: Reprinted by permission from Therese Iknoian, 1995, "Fitness Walking" (Champaign, IL: Human Kinetics Publishers), 32. Call 1-800-747-4457 to order a copy.
Page 128: Reprinted by permission from "Trim Fat from Your Diet—Reduce Risk of Disease" from HealthCheck, a service of O'Bleness Memorial Hospital, Athens, Ohio.
Page 142: From "The Circle of Simplicity" by Cecile Andrews, as excerpted in the *Seattle Times*, February 20, 1997. Copyright © 1997 by Cecile Andrews. Reprinted by permission of HarperCollins Publishers, Inc.
Page 142: The lines from "I thank You God for most this amazing," Copyright © 1950, © 1978, 1991 by the Trustees for the e. e. Cummings Trust. Copyright © 1979 by George J. Firmage from *Complete Poems: 1904–1962* by e. e. Cummings, edited by George J. Firmage. Reprinted by permission of Liveright Publishing Corporation.
Page 172: Reprinted courtesy of Northwest Folklife.
Page 191: Adapted from "Poll Finds Women Favor Dual Roles" by Jay Mathews, *Washington Post*, May 11, 1995, p. B13.

www.hmco.com/college

Printed in the U.S.A.

Library of Congress Catalog Card Number: 97-72517

Student Book ISBN: 0-395-85881-X

4 5 6 7 8 9-CRW-08 07 06 05 04

As part of Houghton Mifflin's ongoing committment to the environment, this text has been printed on recycled paper.

To Anita's father, Robert J. Kain, and to Daphne's parents, Daphne and George Mackey.

Acknowledgments

We would like to thank our families for their support and understanding as we turned our focus to our computers. We are grateful for the feedback of colleagues and students at the University of Washington. In particular, we thank Cara Izumi, Pimporn Chatcharoensuk, Li Ting Wang, Ingak Song, Nipone Jongprasartsuk, Ali Al-Yamani, Hyon-Jeong Park, Eleanor Holstein, Lesley Lin, Jane Power, Jim Ward, and Nancy Ackles, for her knowledge of article use. We also appreciated the comments of reviewers: Victoria Badalamenti, LaGuardia Community College; Brad Beachy, Butler County Community College; Pamela Caywood, San Jose Community College; Peter Clements, ELS Language Center; Kathleen Keesler, Orange Coast College; Roxanne Nuhaily, University of California at San Diego; Dennis Oliver, Arizona State University; Norman Prange, Cayahoga Community College; David Ross, Houston Community College; Kathy Sherak, San Francisco State University; Kay Westerfield, University of Oregon. Thanks also to the people at Houghton Mifflin: Susan Maguire, who brought us on board; Kathy Smith, who kept us on track; and Lauren Wilson, who kept track of everything.

Photo Credits

Contents

Unit 2   The Language of Gestures   *37*

4   Talking without Words   *38*

5   Gestures Around the World   *56*

6   Comfort Zones   *65*

Unit 3   Pets or Pests?   *76*

7   The Great Debate   *77*

8   Pet Therapy   *88*

9   Pet Peeves   *104*

Unit 4   Healthy Choices   *114*

10 Walking   *115*

11 What's on the Menu?   *127*

12 Back to Nature   *137*

KALEIDOSCOPE 2 AT A GLANCE*

Unit	Reading	Preparing to Write	Writing	Targeting Language	Editing & Rewriting
1 New Directions	• context clues (2) • word forms (2) • understanding transitions (3)	• collecting ideas (1) • observing and planning (2) • sentences of introduction and conclusion (2) • brainstorming (3)	• frequently asked questions & answers (1) • description of a place (2) • past travel event (3)	• frequently confused words (2)	• verb forms (1) • present and past tenses (3)
2 The Language of Gestures	• main ideas (4) • context clues (4) • inferences (4) • word forms (4) • diagrams as reading notes (6)	• organizing information (4) • information in instructions (5) • formatting charts (6)	• descriptive article (4) • instructions (5) • recording data results in a chart (6)	• vocabulary for non-verbal greetings (4) • transitions (4) • ways to give instructions (5)	• organization (4) • reading your work aloud (5) • consistent formatting (6)
3 Pets or Pests?	• topics (7) • inference (7) • inference: analyzing cause-effect relationships (8) • word forms (8) • applying information (8) • scanning (9)	• providing supporting ideas (7) • adding specific details (8) • organizing information (9)	• composition with supporting ideas (7) • letter of request (8) • policy memo (9)	• adjectives (7)	• sentence completeness (7) • present perfect tense (8) • singular count nouns (9)
4 Healthy Choices	• analyzing connecting ideas (10) • summarizing (10) • inferences (10) • context clues (10) • diagrams as reading notes (11) • applying information (11)	• organizing information (10) • evaluating with lists (11) • analyzing information (12)	• guidelines and recommendations about an activity (10) • suggestion memo (11) • analysis (12)	• common collocations (12)	• real conditional sentences (10) • non-count nouns (11)

Unit	Reading	Preparing to Write	Writing	Targeting Language	Editing & Rewriting
	• main ideas (12) • paragraph organization (12) • prefixes and roots (12)				
5 Celebrate!	• skimming (13) • reference (14) • scanning (15)	• brainstorming a list (13) • steps to writing a summary (14) • analyzing organization (15) • formal thank-you expressions (15)	• description of a celebration (13) • summary (14) • formal thank-you letter (15)	• ways to describe celebrations (13)	• articles and noun errors in generalizations (13) • appropriate language in formal letters (15)
6 Getting Down to Work	• scanning for topics (16) • summarizing (16) • predicting (17) • words in context (17,18) • scanning (17) • words in context (17,18) • taking notes in a diagram or chart (17) • predicting (18)	• determining the focus (16) • survey (17) • supporting your opinion (18)	• promotional letter (16) • report (17) • Self-evaluation (18)	• expressions for reporting results (17) • transitions that show contrast (18)	• word forms: adjectives and adverbs (16) • verbs in a report (17) • present unreal conditional sentences (18)

*The numbers in parentheses refer to chapters.

Preface

Kaleidoscope 2: Reading and Writing provides low-intermediate students with a variety of tasks designed to improve reading and writing skills. It is based on the following premises:

- Students need more than humanities-based types of writing experiences.
- Students need to develop a working vocabulary within a variety of topics.
- Students need to learn how to edit their own work.

Overview

Kaleidoscope 2 introduces students to the fundamentals of academic, business, technical, and practical writing. *Kaleidoscope 2*

- integrates reading and writing skills.
- focuses on vocabulary development, a key skill in both reading and writing.
- works on key reading skills that help prepare students to deal with authentic texts.
- recycles skills in a variety of ways.
- focuses on multigenre writing.
- includes **Preparing to Write** and **Editing and Rewriting** criteria that help less-experienced instructors feel comfortable with different types of writing assignments.
- uses task-based exercises as much as possible to keep students involved and to reduce the amount of wordiness in the texts.
- allows students to stay within their comfort levels in terms of sharing information and experiences.
- includes ideas for class activities.
- includes a **Reference** section with helpful information such as spelling rules, irregular verb forms, comparatives and superlatives, and formats for formal business letters.

Features

With some variation, the chapters include these main elements and follow this general format:

Starting Point	Connects students to the topic of the chapter.
Reading	Includes reading selection and exercises that focus on comprehension, skill building, and vocabulary.
Targeting	Helps students work with vocabulary, key expressions, and language skills related to a topic or a type of writing.
Writing	Includes Preparing to Write activities that help students develop ideas and write in a variety of formats. The length of compositions has usually been left open in order to fit the curricula of various programs.
Editing and Rewriting	Teaches students how to edit their own writing. It focuses on the most common mistakes in writing and suggests what students ought to look for as they check their work. The Editing Checklist includes questions for peer editing and self-editing.

Additional activities in *Kaleidoscope 2* include Quickwriting and suggestions for Class Activities to round out a topic. Depending on whether class time is used for writing and editing, each chapter will take from one to three hours of class time. Exercises with answers in the back of the book are marked with the (ANSWER KEY) icon.

Training students to be self-editors

Becoming self-editors can be an overwhelming task for ESL students. Therefore, we suggest training students to make multiple passes through their compositions, focusing on one type of error at a time. They will have a better chance of finding errors this way than if they try to find all their mistakes at once. For this reason, each of the *Kaleidoscope 2* editing exercises focuses on one kind of error. As students practice checking for each kind of error in class, encourage them to build up a routine of multiple passes through their work in the editing stage. For example:

- one pass through to look for sentence completeness
- one pass to focus on verb tenses
- another pass to look at nouns: Do they need an article? Do they need to be plural?

As the term progresses, your feedback on their writing will help the students know what kind of errors they should pay most attention to.

Student notebook

We suggest that students use a reading and writing notebook. Possible uses for the notebook include

- quickwriting, as indicated in the text.
- journal writing, if teachers find this activity beneficial.
- keeping track of outside reading with a reading "log" and brief notes about readings—new vocabulary, questions, and interesting ideas.
- reflecting on their progress as writers—what have they learned after completing their work on a topic.

Vocabulary strategies

In order to learn the new vocabulary that they record in their notebooks, they need to use it. Here are some suggestions for additional activities that will help students practice the vocabulary.

- Have students look in newspapers or magazines for vocabulary that they have studied in *Kaleidoscope 2*. Have them write down the sentences they find and share them with the class.
- Have students use the vocabulary in their notebooks and find words from different chapters that could be used in a conversation. Write that conversation.
- Have them find five adjectives from their notebooks and, working in small groups, determine the opposites. Make a matching exercise to give to other groups.
- Look through the vocabulary in their notebooks for words that are related in meaning. Make up related word lists, with one word that doesn't fit. Then write sentences or paragraphs using some of the related words.
- Choose phrasal verbs (with prepositions) or collocations (groups of words that go together) from the vocabulary in their notebooks. Write sentences with these expressions, leaving a blank line for one of the words in the expression. Take turns quizzing the other students on the missing words.
- Use words with short definitions, make flash cards on index cards to practice with or use in a game.

- List nouns from the notebooks and use dictionaries to find the other forms in that word family. Teach these forms to the rest of the class.
- Find words that have the same suffix, prefix, or root. As a class, compile the results in a table.
- Make a drawing to represent a word in their notebooks, and have their classmates guess the word.
- Work in groups to make a crossword puzzle of words from their notebooks. Then exchange puzzles with classmates.
- In a game of word clues, choose words from their notebooks and write them on slips of paper. Working in pairs, each student chooses a word and gives clues about it to his or her partner, who tries to guess the word. After five minutes, change roles or switch partners.
- In group brainstorming, think of synonyms for words from their notebooks. They may use a dictionary. Make a scrambled list of the synonyms and use them for a matching quiz they give to their classmates. Do the same for antonyms.
- Choose five words from the notebooks and survey native speakers for the first word that comes to mind when they hear the target word. Share the word association results with the class.

1 New Directions

There's a lot to learn when you move to any new place. At first, everything is unfamiliar, and it takes time to get adjusted. You have to ask questions, get information, and find your way around.

Here are some activities you will do in this unit:

- Read frequently asked questions about ESL classes
- Exchange information about your area
- Write and answer frequently asked questions
- Read information for newcomers about a city
- Read a map and timetable for public transportation
- Write directions to a place
- Read about an unforgettable travel experience
- Write about a travel experience of your own

Chapter 1

Local Information

What do newcomers need to know? In this chapter you will write frequently asked questions and answers about this kind of information.

Starting Point

What's Difficult for Newcomers?

When you move to a new place, one of the best ways to learn about it is to talk with people.

1. *Here are some things that are often difficult for newcomers. Were they easy or difficult for you when you first arrived? Put a check (✓) on the line under your answer. On the last line, write something else that was difficult or easy for you when you moved to a new place.*

	Easy	Difficult
Finding a place to live	_____	_____
Finding stores	_____	_____
Finding places to eat	_____	_____
Meeting people	_____	_____
Finding places to exercise or play sports	_____	_____
Getting around to see the sights	_____	_____
Using public transportation (bus or subway)	_____	_____
_____ *(your idea)*	_____	_____

2. *Discuss these questions with a partner or a small group.*

   a. When did you move to this area or start to study here?
   b. Discuss your answers in the list in exercise 1. Why were things difficult or easy?

Here is some information for newcomers in an ESL program.

1. *Read the following selection.*

FREQUENTLY ASKED QUESTIONS ABOUT ESL CLASSES

Are ESL classes similar to other classes?

ESL classes are often more student-centered than other classes. Academic lectures, for example, are teacher-centered, but in language classes, students have to practice and do most of the work. An ESL teacher's job is usually to guide students and to give them opportunities for practice and feedback.

Should I call my teacher by the first name or should I use a title and the last name?

Most teachers want you to call them by their first names, but it's all right for you to ask them, "What should I call you? Your first name? Ms./Mr. …?" Usually, only very young children call their teachers "teacher."

If I get to class late, is it all right to enter without asking permission?

You do not need to ask permission to enter the classroom when you are late. Come in the room, but try to be quiet. Try not to interrupt the class. If you want to explain or apologize to the teacher, do this *after* class.

I think that this class is too easy for me. What can I do?

First, talk to your teacher. Students often think a class is going to be easy because teachers usually review things in the first day(s) of class. Teachers like to make sure that students know the basics before they move on to new material. Also, language learning is not like learning math or science. Students have to go over the same verb tenses and the same rules in writing again and again before they learn to use them correctly.

2. *Find the answers to these questions in the reading.*

a. I think I should be in a higher-level class. What should I do

first? _____

_____

b. Is it all right to say, "Teacher," to get your teacher's attention?

_____

c. How are ESL classes different from other classes? _____

_____

d. Why does the class often seem so easy in the first few days?

_____

_____

e. Do I need to apologize to the teacher or ask permission to

enter when I walk into class late? _____

f. How is a language teacher's job different from other

teachers' jobs? _____

_____

3. *In any reading, it's important to learn the new vocabulary and review words you've seen before. Complete these sentences with the correct word(s) in parentheses from the reading.*

a. I often fall asleep during long _____, but I wake up when students have a chance to ask questions. (lectures, classes)

b. My parents _____ me Alison, but everyone

_____ me Ali when I was a little girl. (called, named)

c. The student _____ for being late. She

_____ that her bus was late.
(explained, apologized)

d. The teacher gives students _____ to

_____ English. The students get a lot of

_____ using English outside of class, too.
(opportunities, practice)

e. "That's good" is an example of _____.
(feedback, an answer)

f. Some professors want you to _____ your
questions at the end of class. They don't want you to

_____ the lecture with questions.
(ask, interrupt)

g. Last night I _____ all my grammar notes. I

read the rules a lot, but I need to _____
more.   (practice(d), review(ed))

4. *Look at the reading "Frequently Asked Questions about ESL
Classes." For each sentence below, find a word or an expression
in the reading that has the same meaning as the word(s) in
parentheses. Write the word or expression in the blank.*

(ANSWER KEY)

a. I need to (review) _____ the vocabulary we
studied last week.

b. Please (check, be careful) _____ that you
have your name on your homework.

c. Students need to know the (most elementary things)

_____ before they move on to more
difficult things.

Writing

Preparing to Write: Collecting Ideas

What kind of information could *you* provide to newcomers? Your writing assignment will be to write information for newcomers. The first step is to collect ideas and decide on your topic.

1. *With a partner or a small group, think about what you needed to know when you were a newcomer to your area or program. Study the examples.*

   About Your Area
   how to open a bank account
   the cheapest stores for school and kitchen supplies

   About Studying in Your Program
   ways to practice and improve my English
   ways to meet native speakers
   differences about studying in this program

   Now, make a list of your ideas.

   _____

   _____

   _____

   _____

   _____

   _____

   _____

   _____

2. *Make a list of questions that a newcomer might ask. Be sure that you include enough questions to cover all the topics you listed in exercise 1.*

   _____

   _____

_____

_____

_____

Now that you have developed some ideas, you are ready to write.

Create an information sheet below for newcomers to your area or program. Use the format of Frequently Asked Questions and Answers. Choose three of your most interesting questions from exercise 2 in Preparing to Write.

- _____

_____

_____

- _____

_____

_____

- _____

_____

_____

Writing Frequently Asked Questions and Answers

WRITING TIP

Think about your audience—newcomers to the area or program. Do the answers to your questions give enough information? Also, think about a way to make the questions easy to see. For example, highlight them or separate them from the answers.

Editing and Rewriting

Editing for Verb Forms

It's a good idea to check your verbs every time you write. Make sure they agree with their subjects.

1. *Study these rules.*

Rules	Examples
The third person singular in the present tense always has an **-s.** The spelling of the **-s** ending may be **-s, -es,** or **-ies.**	The new program start**s** in September. He teach**es** English. She stud**ies** in the library. The lecture class **has** 200 students in it.
The subject of the sentence is not always right next to the verb.	*One* of the buildings **is** quite old. *Some* of the buildings **are** newer.
The subject follows "There **is/are/was/were.**"	There **was** a lot of *traffic.* There **were** a lot of *cars.* There **were** *two cars and a truck* on the side of the road.
Modals are followed by the base form of the verb.	**have to** **should** + study (base form) **ought to**
To form a question in the present, use *do/does, is/are,* or a modal with the base form of the verb.	Where **is** a drugstore? How much **does** it **cost** to take the bus? Where **can** I **buy** a newspaper?

For more information about the spelling of verb endings, see Reference page 216.

2. *Put a check (✓) in front of the sentence(s) with correct verb forms.*

ANSWER KEY

a. _____ The restaurant serves food twenty-four hours a day.

b. _____ There was problems with his directions to the restaurant. We got lost.

c. _____ One of the stores downtown sell food from my country.

d. _____ You should try it sometime.

e. _____ There aren't any Armenian restaurants here.

f. _____ One of the people in my class is from Greece.

3. *Underline the subjects and correct the errors in the verbs in the following sentences. The first one has been done for you.*

ANSWER KEY

a. Where can I ~~to get~~ *get* the bus?

b. The bus leave every fifteen minutes.

c. He must pays when he gets on the bus.

d. Where is the best places to eat?

e. One of the best restaurants are the University Grill.

f. You should to try the Deli Express.

g. The bus ride take twenty minutes.

h. At the Crosstown Mall, there is a lot of ethnic restaurants.

i. Where are the best place for a student to buy notebooks and things like that?

j. You should to try the discount office supply stores.

k. An office supply store have lots of things for students.

l. A drugstore also sell inexpensive supplies for students.

Editing Checklist

Check the Content

1. *Exchange your newcomer information sheet with a classmate. After you read what your classmate wrote, answer these questions.*

   ❑ Are the questions easy to understand?
   ❑ Do the answers give newcomers enough information?

Check the Details

2. *Now, reread your own information sheet. If necessary, revise what you wrote. Give more information or make it clearer. Then continue checking your own writing. Use these questions.*

   ❑ Do any verbs need an **-s** ending?
   ❑ If there are modals, does the base form of the verb follow them?
   ❑ Did you use **is/are, do/does**, or a modal with the base form for your questions?
   ❑ Does every sentence begin with a capital letter and end with a period, a question mark, or an exclamation point?

3. *Make your corrections and rewrite your information sheet.*

Vocabulary Log

While you are using this book, keep a notebook. Use this notebook to list and review vocabulary and grammar as well as for your writing. What words or phrases would you like to remember from this chapter? Write five to ten items in your notebook. Be sure to write other forms of the word that you know or words that go with it, such as prepositions. Also write a sentence so that you will remember how to use each word or phrase. Here are a couple of examples:

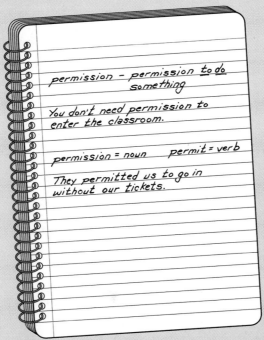

How can you learn the words you list? Is there anything else that you would like to add to the information in your notebook? Discuss with a classmate and/or your teacher.

Grammar and Punctuation Review

Look over your writing from this chapter. What changes did you need to make in grammar and punctuation? Write your errors and the corrected sentences in your notebook. Then use the correct grammar or punctuation again in new sentences. Review them before the next writing assignment.

Class Activity An Exhibit for Newcomers

Think about your writing from this chapter. Would it be helpful to newcomers to your area or school? If so, put the information in a brochure or put together an exhibit that gives newcomers information about your area or school. Add some photos. Display the exhibit in a place where newcomers will see it.

Chapter 2

New to the City

Reading about a new place helps you get to know it. In this chapter you will read about a new city and study vocabulary that is often confusing to newcomers.

Starting Point

Seeing the local sights is a good way to find out about a new area.

Seeing the Local Sights

Look at the photograph. Discuss these questions with a partner or a small group.

1. What city or country do you think this photograph is from?

2. Write six words that describe the place in the photograph.

_____   _____

_____   _____

_____   _____

3. Is the place similar to or different from places you are familiar with? Explain your answers.

_____

_____

_____

_____

_____

_____

_____

_____

_____

_____

Reading

....

A Newcomer's Guide to New Orleans

This selection gives a newcomer ideas for a tour of the French Quarter—the old section of New Orleans.

1. _Read the following selection._

A Newcomer's Guide to New Orleans

[1] The city of New Orleans is on the Mississippi River in the state of Louisiana. Originally French, New Orleans is very different from other cities in the United States. A favorite tourist destination, New Orleans is also a busy port and home to about 500,000 people.

[2] At the heart of New Orleans is the French Quarter, also known as the _Vieux Carré_. The French Quarter has some of the oldest buildings in the city, as well as lovely houses, famous restaurants, and exciting jazz clubs.

[3] Start your tour of the French Quarter with a _café au lait_ and _beignets_ (a type of pastry) at the Café du Monde. _Du Monde_ means "of the world," and you really feel as if you see people from all over the

world when you sit there. Then walk across the street to Jackson Square, a lovely park. There you can listen to street musicians and watch artists who spend the day entertaining the tourists around the square.

[4] Stand in the center of the square and look around you. In one direction you will see St. Louis Cathedral and the Cabildo, a historical museum. On two sides are the red brick Pontalba Buildings, the oldest apartment buildings in the United States. In the other direction you will see huge freighters, casino gambling ships, and tour boats all pass on the Mississippi River.

[5] Walk along Royal Street to visit the art galleries and antique shops. Walk along Chartres Street or Ursuline Avenue and look at the beautiful old houses with balconies full of flowers. Eat lunch or dinner at any of the famous restaurants in the Quarter, but be sure to check the prices on the menus outside the doors—they can be expensive. After dinner, join hundreds of other tourists who walk along Bourbon Street and watch the night life.

The next exercises help you use **context** to guess meanings.

2. *Answer these questions about the new vocabulary in the reading. Then, in the reading, underline the words or expressions that gave you the answer. The first one has been done for you.*

    a. Is New Orleans a city or a state? _A city_

    b. Is Louisiana a city or a state? _____

    c. Was New Orleans always part of the United States? _____

> **READING TIP**
>
> You don't always need to look up new words in a dictionary. The **context** can help you guess the meanings of unfamiliar words.

    d. What is another name for the French Quarter? _____

    e. What is a *beignet*? _____

    f. What does *du Monde* mean? _____

    g. What is Jackson Square? _____

    h. What is the Cabildo? _____

    i. What are the Pontalba Buildings? _____

Reflect on Reading

Punctuation marks can be clues to the meanings of words. In "A Newcomer's Guide to New Orleans," the use of italics, parentheses, quotation marks, and the comma helps the reader to define words.

Look at paragraph 3 in the reading. Then complete the following sentences with one of these words or expressions.

parentheses ( )   italics *italics*   quotation marks " "   a comma ,

1. _____ shows that a word is foreign.

2. Either _____ or _____ can be used to show more information about something.

3. _____ shows a definition.

3. *Find the places on this map that are mentioned in "A Newcomer's Guide to New Orleans." Draw a line to show where the reading suggests that newcomers walk.*

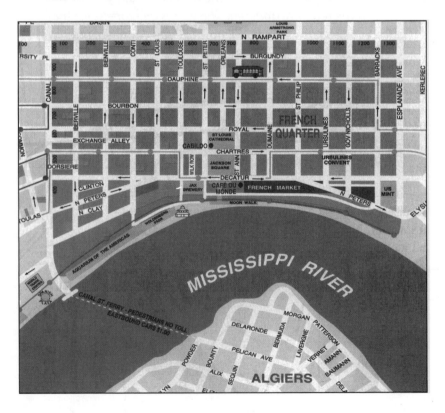

If you know common endings for different word forms, you can improve your reading skills. For example, if you know the word *move* ("We moved the chairs into a circle."), you can probably understand these other sentences.

> When we moved to New York, we didn't pack everything ourselves. *Movers* packed for us.

> In a small apartment, easily *moveable* furniture is great.

4. *Find words in the reading to complete this chart.*

ANSWER KEY

Base Form	Person	Adjective
music		musical
art		artistic
tour		
history	historian	
beauty		

Targeting

In this section you will learn about some common words and expressions that people often confuse.

Frequently Confused Words

1. *Study these rules.*

Words	Rules	Examples
another, other(s)	Which of these two words you must use depends on how many you are talking about.	There are several bookstores. One sells children's books. **Another** sells books for tourists. (You are talking about *one* of *many*.) Some restaurants serve French food. **Others** serve a variety of foods. (You are talking about one of two groups— *French restaurants* and *all the rest*.)

Words	Rules	Examples
the other(s)	*The other(s)* means the rest of the group or pair, the one(s) that remain(s).	There are two cafés in that block. One serves French pastries. **The other** doesn't. I always go to this restaurant because it is inexpensive. I never go to **the others.**

Note: Be careful about your punctuation with these words.
There are two big roads near my house. One is quiet and the other is noisy.
NOT:
There are two big roads near my house, one is quiet and the other is noisy.

Words	Rules	Examples
most *most of*	Both of these mean *more than 50 percent.*	
	Most describes a general, nonspecific noun.	**Most** restaurants are open for lunch and dinner.
	Most of describes a specific noun or a pronoun.	**Most of the** restaurants downtown are open for lunch and dinner. (This refers to the specific restaurants downtown.) **Most of them** serve dinner until 10 p.m. (Again, the expression refers to the restaurants downtown.) **Most of the food** is excellent. (*The* food at the restaurants downtown—specific.)
almost	*Almost* means nearly. Almost is *NEVER* followed directly by a noun.	**Almost all** of the restaurants are open on Sunday. NOT: Almost restaurants are open on Sunday. I'm **almost** finished. We **almost** got tickets to the game. We **almost always** eat lunch at 12:30.

2. *Use the words in the chart from exercise 1 to complete these sentences about music clubs in New Orleans. There may be more than one possible answer.* ANSWER KEY

a. Mardi Gras is a big celebration in New Orleans that a lot of people come to see. _____*Another*_____ celebration that brings visitors is the Jazz Festival.

b. Some people go to New Orleans to see the old buildings and tourist sites. _____ go to New Orleans because they love music.

c. Some visitors spend _____ their nights at clubs listening to music.

d. _____ bars in the French Quarter have live music, not taped music.

e. There are a lot of places in New Orleans to listen to jazz. Preservation Hall is famous in the French Quarter for its traditional jazz. _____ place that plays traditional jazz is the Palm Court Jazz Café.

f. _____ people who go to New Orleans visit Preservation Hall.

g. _____ the music clubs open at 8:00 or 9:00 p.m.

h. _____ all of the clubs stay open late at night.

i. I visited two jazz clubs when I was in New Orleans. One was called Snug Harbor. _____ was the New Showcase Lounge. Both had great jazz!

j. There are a lot of clubs where you can dance. One of my

favorites is Tipitina's. _____ is the Maple

Leaf.

k. You can hear street musicians at _____ any

time of the day or night in Jackson Square.

3. *Write sentences about the area where you live. Use the words in the chart from exercise 1 on pages 17–18.*

_____

_____

_____

_____

_____

Writing

Preparing to Write 1: Observing

What places near your classroom would a newcomer be interested in? Before you write a description of that place, it's a good idea to look at the place and take some notes.

1. *With a partner, choose an interesting place near your classroom. (Your teacher may have some suggestions.) Go to that place. Take your notebooks.*

2. *Take notes about this place. Do not write sentences at this time. Just write all of your observations and feelings about the place. Here are some things to think about.*

   What do you see? Is there a view? Is the place or room interesting to look at?
   What smells and sounds do you notice?
   What kinds of things or people do you see here? What are they doing?
   What or who does this place make you think of?
   How do you feel in this place?

3. *You may want to make a sketch or a diagram of the place to help you remember how it looks.*

Once you have some information about your topic, you need to decide which information to include in your description.

1. *Look at your notes from your visit to an interesting place. Which information would be the most interesting to someone who is unfamiliar with this place?*

2. *You need a sentence to introduce your reader to your information. Here are some possibilities.*

   > *. . . is a . . . place to . . . , visit/study/have a cup of coffee. . . .*
   > Yesterday, I visited. . . . It was. . . .
   > You should definitely pay a visit to. . . .
   > Don't miss the . . . when you are. . . .
   > If you are . . . , stop by the. . . .

   *Write your **introductory sentence** here.*

   _____

   _____

> **WRITING TIP**
>
> Once again, think about your audience —newcomers to the area. What information will they be interested in?

3. *Go back to your notes. Underline the information that you will include in your description. What will you write about first, second, and so on?*

4. *You will also need a sentence of **conclusion** to end your description. Look at the sentences in exercise 2 for an idea. Write your ending sentence here.*

   _____

   _____

Now it's time to put it all together.

Write a description of the place you visited.

Writing a Description of a Place

In English, the first sentence of a paragraph usually begins three to five spaces to the right of the other lines. This is called **indenting.** Always **indent** your paragraphs.

Editing and Rewriting

Editing Checklist

Check the Content

1. *Exchange your description with a classmate. After you read your classmate's description, answer these questions.*

   ❏ Is there a sentence of introduction and a sentence of conclusion?
   ❏ Is there enough information? Do you know what the place is like?
   ❏ Are the ideas in an order that is easy to follow?

Check the Details

2. *Now, reread your own description. Keep in mind the questions in exercise 1. If necessary, revise what you wrote. Add sentences at the beginning or end. Give more information, or make your description clearer. Then continue checking your own writing. Use these questions.*

   ❏ Do any verbs need an **-s** ending?
   ❏ If there are modals, do the base forms of the verb follow them?
   ❏ Is your paragraph indented?
   ❏ Does every sentence begin with a capital letter and end with a period, a question mark, or an exclamation point?

3. *Make your corrections and rewrite your description.*

Vocabulary Log

What words or phrases would you like to remember from this chapter? Write five to ten items in your notebook. Examples are on page 11.

Grammar and Punctuation Review

Look over your writing from this chapter. What changes did you need to make in grammar and punctuation? Write them in your notebook. Review them before the next writing assignment.

Chapter 3

Getting There

Getting from one place to another is often challenging. Accurate information, maps, and schedules are especially important. In this chapter you will read maps and schedules as well as a story of a difficult travel experience. You will also write about your own travel experience.

Starting Point

Getting Around

Discuss these questions with a partner or a small group.

> How do you get to class?
> Is it easy or difficult for you?

Reading 1

A Map and a Timetable

Reading a map and a timetable is very important if you need to take public transportation.

1. *Look at the map. Then answer the questions about the bus routes.*

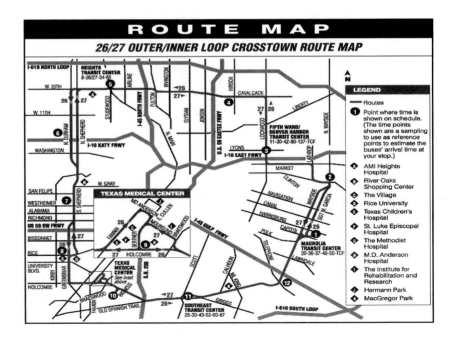

a. What is the basic difference between route #26 and route #27?

_____

_____

b. What do the numbers in circles show? _____

_____

c. What do the letters in diamonds show? _____

_____

2. *Look at the timetable for the bus route in exercise 1. Answer these questions about the bus schedule.*

Route 27—Weekday Schedule

①	⑫	⑪	⑩	⑨	⑧
4:50 a	5:00 a	5:11 a	5:24 a	5:33 a	5:46 a
5:15	5:25	5:36	5:49	5:58	6:11
5:30	5:40	5:51	6:04	6:13	6:26
5:45	5:55	6:06	6:19	6:28	6:41
6:00	6:10	6:21	6:34	6:43	6:56
6:15	6:25	6:36	6:49	6:58	7:11
6:30	6:40	6:51	7:04	7:13	7:26
6:45	6:55	7:06	7:19	7:28	7:41
7:00	7:10	7:21	7:34	7:43	7:56
7:15	7:25	7:36	7:49	7:58	8:11

a. What does the *a* next to the first times probably mean?

_____

b. Look at the timetable and the route map. What are the numbers across the top of the timetable?

_____

c. How long does it take to get from stop 11 to stop 10?

_____

d. Arturo Rodriquez lives near the Magnolia Transit Center. He works at Texas Children's Hospital. His hours are 6:30 a.m. to

> **READING TIP**
>
> When you read a timetable, always read from left to right. Look at the top row first to find the column for the information you need.

3:30 p.m. What time does he need to catch a bus in the morning?

_____

e. Arturo's daughter goes to Rice University. Her first class is at 8:00 a.m. What time does she need to catch a bus in the morning?

_____

Reflect on Reading

In this section you read a city map and a timetable for a bus. Do you need to read maps or timetables outside of class? What makes them easy or difficult to read? Discuss this with a partner or a small group.

How's Your Daily Commute to the University?

Traffic is always a problem, especially when 8,000 people need to get to the university area every day. We decided to ask some of the people who work here at the university about their commutes.

Jack Loring (doctor):
I work across the lake from my home, but the traffic on the bridge across the lake is terrible. Sometimes it's just like a parking lot. When the weather is good, I take my boat across the lake and then walk to the university hospital. It sure beats driving.

Peter Jefferson (int'l student advisor):
I live near the university, so I usually ride my bicycle to work or walk. I hate walking at night though, especially if it's raining. A car hit me one night when I was crossing the street. I was lucky because I wasn't hurt very badly.

Sarah Schmidt (teacher):
I live on an island, so I park my car at the ferry dock and get on a passenger ferry. The thirty minute ferry ride is very relaxing but then I have a thirty minute bus ride. The bus doesn't stop near my office, so I have to walk for another twenty-five minutes! We're thinking about moving.

Carla Thompson (administrator):
I live south of the airport. I used to take the bus to work, but it took too long and didn't stop near my office. Now I drive, and the traffic is terrible—especially on Friday afternoons. Sometimes it takes an hour and a half to get home. I often think about moving.

Ingrid Sundstren (student):
I live in the dormitory, so I walk to class every day. It only takes me about ten minutes, but I hate it when it's raining! The funny thing is that I often arrive later than students who come to class by bus. There's often a line in the cafeteria for breakfast, and I never leave enough time.

There are lots of ways to get to work. Some people spend hours on their commute. Others spend only minutes.

How's Your Daily Commute?

1. *Read the newspaper clipping on page 26.*

2. *Match the transportation with the people. Put checks (✓) under the names. You will use more than one check for some people.*

	Jack	*Peter*	*Sarah*	*Carla*	*Ingrid*
takes the bus					
rides a bicycle					
walks					
rides a boat or ferry					
drives					

3. *Read the article again. It doesn't tell you exactly where these people live, but you can infer it from the context. Write their names on the map.*

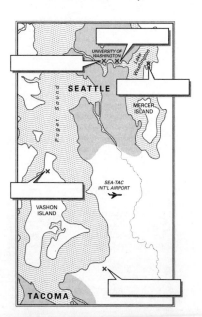

4. *Each person in the article mentions a problem. List each one's problem(s) here.*

Jack: _____

_____

Peter: _____

_____

Sarah: _____

_____

Carla: _____

_____

Ingrid: _____

_____

5. *What do* **you** *think about these ways of getting to work or school? What do you think are the advantages and disadvantages of public transportation? Complete the chart.*

	Advantages	*Disadvantages*
car		
public transportation		

6. *Read "How's Your Daily Commute?" again and study the vocabulary. Underline all the words and expressions in the reading that are related to transportation. List them in your notebook. With a partner or in a small group, discuss the similarities and differences in meaning.*

Reading 3

....

Travel can be very stressful. Some people have difficult travel experiences they will never forget.

1. *Read "An Unforgettable Travel Experience." Then number these pictures in the order that they happened. The first one has been done for you.*

An Unforgettable Travel Experience

1

An Unforgettable Travel Experience

[1] My trip to the United States was a terrible experience, one that I will never forget! **My first problem** was the food on the airplane. I am a vegetarian, and there was almost nothing for me to eat for almost twenty-four hours. I didn't realize that you could order special meals in advance for an airplane trip.

[2] I had arranged everything through a travel agent in my country. Unfortunately, I only told the travel agent, "I'm going to the University of Washington." She didn't know much about the United States. I was supposed to go to Seattle, Washington. **Instead,** I arrived in Washington, D.C. Can you imagine how I felt?

[3] **The next day** I was able to fly to Seattle. **However,** I had to change planes in Chicago, and my suitcases didn't arrive in Seattle on my plane. **As a result,** I had no extra clothes and no toothbrush for the first days!

[4] I went to the hotel where I had reservations, **but** there was no longer a room for me **because** I was a day late. When I called the university, I started crying. I felt like going back home!

2. *Look at the transition words and expressions in **boldface** in the reading. Decide what they show. Then write them in one of the columns in the chart.*

ANSWER KEY

Transitions That Show Sequence	Transitions That Show Contrast	Transitions That Show Cause or Result
My first problem	_____	_____
_____	_____	_____
	_____	

3. *Are these sentences true or false? Write **T** or **F** on the lines.*

ANSWER KEY

a. _T_ The writer traveled by plane.

b. _____ She made the reservations herself.

c. _____ The trip to Washington State took twenty-four hours.

d. _____ She was hungry because there was no food served on the plane.

e. _____ She called the hotel from Washington, D.C. and changed her reservation.

f. _____ Her suitcases were lost between Washington, D.C., and Seattle.

4. *People often use the expression **"It's _____ to _____ . . ."** to respond to people's experiences. Comment on "An Unforgettable Travel Experience." Complete the sentences with words from the list. Some words are used more than once.*

ANSWER KEY

It's	a good idea	to	believe . . .
	fun		check . . .
	hard		keep . . .
	important		remember . . .
	impossible		tell . . .

a. It's ____hard____ to ____believe____ one person had so many problems!

b. It's _____ to _____ your plane ticket information before you leave.

c. This story is _____ to _____, but it's true!

d. It's _____ to _____ a change of clothes and a toothbrush with you on the airplane.

e. It's usually _____ to _____ everything when you are very busy.

f. When she is an old woman, she will laugh at this experience.

It will be _____ to _____ her story to people.

Writing

Preparing to Write: Brainstorming About Travel Experiences

One of the hardest parts of writing is coming up with ideas. One technique for coming up with ideas is **brainstorming.** When you brainstorm, you talk or write notes about as many things as possible.

1. *What unforgettable travel experiences have you had? They can be pleasant or difficult. Think of your experiences with any kind of travel: by air, boat, car, bus, or on foot. Write some notes about them.*

    _____

    _____

    _____

    _____

    _____

2. *Now go back and look at your notes. What made these experiences interesting? Add more information to your notes. See the example below.*

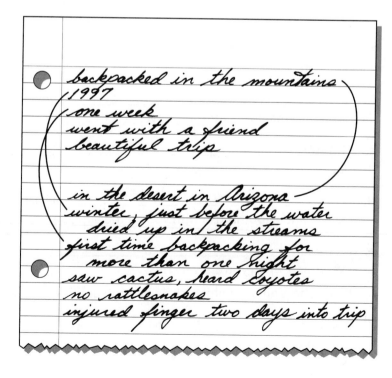

Choose one of your travel experiences and write about it. Be sure to include the most interesting details in your story.

WRITING TIP

Be sure to use the past tense for experiences finished in the past.

Editing and Rewriting

It's important to check your work for the correct verb tense.

1. *Review the rules in the box.*

Editing for Present and Past Tense

Rules	Examples
Use the present tense for *habits, facts,* and *general truths.*	Kim always **catches** the express bus when he **goes** downtown. The express bus usually **takes** thirty minutes.
Use the simple past tense for *events that happened in the past* and *are finished.*	Yesterday, Maria **caught** the bus at the first stop. Last week, she **took** the wrong bus by mistake.

For more information about the spelling of verb endings, see Reference page 216. For more information about past tense verbs, see Reference page 214.

2. *Go back to "An Unforgettable Travel Experience" on page 30. Underline the verbs that are **not** in the past tense. Now, work with a partner. Can you explain why they are not in the past tense?*

ANSWER KEY

_____   _____

_____   _____

_____   _____

ANSWER KEY

3. *Practice using the correct verb tense. Complete the sentences with the present or past form of the verb in parentheses.*

My brother usually (have) _____ no
(a)

problem getting home, but one time he (have) _____
(b)

a very difficult time getting home on the bus. This semester he

(have) _____ classes on Tuesday and
(c)

Thursday, so he (have to) _____ go
(d)

downtown twice a week. He always (take) _____ the
(e)

express bus because it (be) _____ faster
(f)

than the local bus.

Sometimes, when he (get) _____ on the bus, he (fall)
(g)

_____ asleep. Last week, he (get)
(h)

_____ on the bus and immediately (fall)
(i)

_____ asleep. He (wake) _____ up
(j)   (k)

when the bus (stop) _____ .
(l)

However, he (have) _____ no idea
(m)

where he (be) _____ . He (be) _____ on
(n)   (o)

the wrong express bus! Unfortunately, there (be) _____

(p)

no buses going in the opposite direction until the next morning.

He (have to) _____ take a taxi to get home.

(q)

That (turn out) _____ to be a very expensive day!

(r)

Editing Checklist

Check the Content

1. *Exchange your description of a travel experience with a classmate. After you read what your classmate wrote, answer the question.*

   ❏ Are there enough details for readers to understand the story clearly?

2. *Write sentences about your classmate's story using the structure "It's . . . to . . . " If necessary, review exercise 4 on page 31.*

   _____

   _____

   _____

   _____

Check the Details

3. *Now, reread your own story. If necessary, revise what you wrote. Add more details. Then continue checking your own writing. Use these questions.*

   ❏ Check every verb. Is the past tense used for things that happened in the past?
   ❏ Do you need an *-s* ending for the third person singular in the present tense?
   ❏ Did you begin every sentence with a capital letter and end with a period, a question mark, or an exclamation point?

4. *Make your corrections and rewrite your story.*

Vocabulary Log

What words or phrases would you like to remember from this chapter? Write five to ten items in your notebook. Examples are on page 11.

Grammar and Punctuation Review

Look over your writing from this chapter. What changes did you need to make in grammar and punctuation? Write them in your notebook. Review them before the next writing assignment.

2 The Language of Gestures

We communicate in many ways without words. We use our hands, facial expressions, and body language. This unit features nonverbal communication.

Here are some activities you will do in this unit:

- Read a definition
- Read descriptions of greetings
- Write a description of a greeting
- Write instructions
- Present data in a chart

Chapter 4

Talking without Words

In what ways do we communicate without speaking? This chapter is about different kinds of nonverbal communication, especially greeting customs. After you read about greeting customs in other cultures, you will write a description of nonverbal greetings in your country.

Starting Point

Gestures

A lot of our communication is without words. We call this **nonverbal communication.**

1. *With a classmate, practice these conversations nonverbally. Try to communicate the ideas in parentheses. You may only use gestures. Then compare your conversations with other classmates' conversations.*

   Conversation 1
Student A:	(Student B has a telephone call.)
Student B:	(I can't come to the phone because I am eating.)
Student A:	(I don't know what to do.)
Student B:	(I'll call back later.)

   Conversation 2
Student A:	(I feel cold.)
Student B:	(Do you want a sweater?)
Student A:	(Yes, I want a sweater.)
Student B:	(I will get one.)

2. *We use many unspoken greetings. Study the following pictures of people greeting each other. Complete the phrases that describe the pictures with words or expressions from the list. The first one has been done for you.*

smile	eye contact	kiss	shake hands
cheek	pat	someone's	back
hug	bow		

a.

to _____*kiss*_____ someone on the _____*cheek*_____

b.

to _____ someone or each other

c.

to _____ slightly to someone

d.

to _____ someone on the _____

e.

to _____ or to shake _____ hand

f.

to _____ and make _____ with someone

Reading 1

Nonverbal Communication

How much of our communication is nonverbal? How many different ways are there to communicate nonverbally?

1. *Read the following selection.*

Nonverbal Communication

[1] People talk a lot, but about 60 percent of all our communication is nonverbal (without words). There are about 700,000 ways to communicate nonverbally. For about a third of those ways we use our faces. Our eyes, eyebrows, noses, mouths, and eyelids can say a lot. We also use at least 5,000 hand gestures. The third way we communicate nonverbally is through body movement—the way we sit or stand, and even how far we stand from someone.

[2] Gestures have different purposes. They give instructions or warnings. For example, if you hold up the palm of your hand toward someone, it means "Don't come here!" or "Stay back!" Gestures also communicate warmth. A smile means "I like you" or "Welcome." A handshake says "Hello." Finally, body language, such as a thumb pointing down or a frown, can express negative feelings.

[3] Although gestures are easy to make, they can be very confusing across cultures. For example, in the United States, it's polite to look people in the eye when you talk to them. This look says, "I am listening to you" and "I am honest." However, in many Asian countries, it is impolite to look someone in the eye.

In English, each paragraph focuses on one topic. What the writer has to say about the topic is the main idea.

2. *Write the paragraph numbers next to the listed topics from "Nonverbal Communication."*

   a. _____   meanings of gestures

   b. _____   body language around the world

   c. _____   types of gestures

3. *What is the author's main point about each topic? Circle the best main idea for each paragraph.*

   a. Paragraph 1
      1. People talk a lot, but most of the talking is nonverbal.
      2. There are thousands of ways to communicate with gestures.
      3. There are three main types of nonverbal communication.

b. Paragraph 2

     1. Gestures express unhappiness as well as warmth.

     2. Nonverbal communication can communicate different feelings.

     3. The most common purpose of gestures is to give instructions or warnings.

   c. Paragraph 3

     1. Gestures do not always communicate the same thing in different countries.

     2. It's not always polite to look people in the eye when you are talking to them.

     3. In Asian countries, it is impolite to make eye contact.

4. *What topic connects these words? Circle the word or phrase that is the most general. The first one has been done for you.*

    a. nonverbal   verbal   (communication)   gestures

    b. eyes   face   eyebrows   eyelids

    c. palm   hand   fingers   thumb

    d. happiness   friendliness   anger   feelings

    e. facial gestures   smiling   eyebrows raised   winking

    f. shaking hands   bowing   patting someone on the back   body language

Reflect on Reading

You found the **main idea** in exercise 3. The main idea is what the writer wants to communicate about the topic. Sometimes the writer expresses a feeling or an attitude about a topic. This feeling or attitude may or may not be directly stated. The main idea is a general idea that covers all of the details in the paragraph or reading.

In which of these situations would finding the main idea be important? Discuss with a partner or a small group.

Reading want ads in a newspaper

Reading a textbook for a course

Reading a biography of a famous person

5. *Circle the number of the best response.*

   a. According to the reading, which of the following is *not* true?

      1. Gestures communicate many things.
      2. More than half of our communication is done without talking.
      3. Gestures are the same around the world.
      4. Thirty percent of all gestures are facial gestures.

   b. Nonverbal communication _____.

      1. is not polite
      2. is the same from culture to culture
      3. uses thirty facial expressions
      4. includes how we stand

   c. It is not polite to look someone in the eye _____.

      1. in a lot of countries
      2. in a lot of countries in Asia
      3. in the United States
      4. only in the United States

6. *Use your knowledge from reading "Nonverbal Communication" and the clues within these paragraphs to complete the last sentences. Circle the number of the answer.*

   a. In the United States, it's important to maintain eye contact in job interviews. Eye contact can have a big effect on the interviewer. It shows that you are interested in him or her and that you are an honest person. For this reason, applicants who do not make eye contact _____.

      1. often get the job
      2. do not often get the job
      3. are not honest people

   b. Appearance also communicates a lot to a potential employer. This can mean how you dress and how you hold yourself (your posture) when you are sitting or standing. If you are clean and your clothes are neat, you show that you are a careful person. What you wear also tells people how you feel. If you are dressed too casually, you will look as if you don't care about the job. On the other hand, if you are overdressed, it will appear that you are trying too hard or that you are not aware of appropriate clothes for work. A person who stands too straight may appear too formal. On the other hand, a person who does not sit up straight in the chair _____.

  1. appears too relaxed
  2. seems not to care about the job
  3. appears too formal

c. Psychologists studying nonverbal communication often videotape people telling real stories and made-up ones. Then others have to decide when the person is lying. They usually figure out who is lying about half of the time if the person is from their own culture. It is much harder to detect a lie if _____.

  1. the person is not telling the truth
  2. the person is making up stories
  3. the person comes from a different culture

d. Although some people are very successful liars, most of us have a hard time lying to people we know. This is because it is difficult to hide nonverbal communication for very long. Our eyes give us away when we are not telling the truth. One way to tell if someone is lying is to watch the pupils of his or her eyes. When the person is preparing the lie, the black part of the eye will get small. On the contrary, while the person is actually telling the lie, _____.

  1. the pupils will get large
  2. the person will look away
  3. the person will look down

e. Complete silence is also a form of nonverbal communication, but what does it communicate? Most of the time in the United States, a long silence has a negative meaning. Usually, when people look at you with a blank face and are silent, it means they do not agree with you or may even be angry with you. However, they are not disagreeing or angry with you if _____.

  1. they are making gestures
  2. they are keeping eye contact
  3. they are also smiling

7. *Match the opposites of vocabulary from exercise 6. Write the numbers on the lines.*

ANSWER KEY

a. __5__ interviewer   **1.** telling the truth

b. _____ real   **2.** give (oneself) away

c. _____ casually   **3.** (sitting up) straight

d. _____ formal   **4.** made-up

e. _____ lying   **5.** applicant

f. _____ hide   **6.** formally

g. _____ relaxed posture   **7.** relaxed

8. *Sometimes you can understand the meaning of words from the* **context** *(see pages 15–16 in Chapter 2). Find words or explanations in the paragraphs in exercise 6 that help you understand these words. Write them here.*

ANSWER KEY

a. lying   _____*not telling the truth*_____

b. pupils _____

c. appearance _____

d. posture _____

e. detect _____

Quickwriting: Nonverbal Communication and You

Are you a demonstrative person? Do you use a lot of gestures when you speak, or do you let the words do all of the talking? In your notebook, write for five to ten minutes about yourself and nonverbal communication. Write as quickly as you can. Don't worry about spelling, grammar, or punctuation. If you don't know a word in English, write it in your own language.

Reading 2

Trusty Travel Tips

Trusty Travel Tips, a popular travel guide, includes a chapter on greeting gestures.

1. *Read these descriptions of greetings in Thailand and Turkey from* ***Trusty Travel Tips.***

Thailand

[1] If you travel to Thailand, you will have to know about the ***wai.*** This is the most important greeting. To make the *wai,* put your two hands together with the thumbs in front of your chest. You make the *wai* and bow your head slightly to a relative, a teacher, or an older person. It is a sign of respect. You do not make eye contact while you do this. However, greeting a friend is different. You only need to smile and make eye contact to say "Hello."

[2] When you are in Thailand, you may see some men shaking hands. This is the Western influence. Be very careful about shaking hands. In general, people do not touch when they greet each other. There is no kissing on the cheek, hugging, or patting on the back. Each of these acts of touching is impolite. Thai people are very friendly but also very careful about polite nonverbal communication.

Turkey

[1] Most greetings in Turkey are similar to those of other Eastern European cultures. Friends and family members of the same sex or opposite sex usually kiss each other on both cheeks to say "Hello." If you are just acquaintances or meeting for the first time, you will shake hands—even with a woman if she extends her hand first.

[2] There is one gesture, however, that connects Turkey to the Middle East and its Islamic roots. In Islamic tradition, it is very important to respect people who are older and, therefore, more knowledgeable. The most interesting way to greet an older person is ***el öpmek*** (to kiss the hand). This gesture is only used to show great respect to a man or

woman who is older than you. To make this gesture, take the older person's right hand (palm side down) lightly in your right hand. Then kiss the back of the hand gently and place it against your own forehead.

[3] With this greeting, you show how much you like this older person and appreciate his or her wisdom. Some people perform *el öpmek* routinely, that is, without really thinking about the meaning. For example, the older person may automatically move his or her hand to the younger person's forehead. This is not the best way to perform this greeting. If this gesture is made sincerely, it can be a deeply touching moment.

2. *You can **infer** from the reading if the following sentences are true or false. The author doesn't tell you directly. Put a **T** next to the true statements and an **F** next to the false statements.*

a. ___F___ The *wai* is a greeting between friends.

b. _____ Husband and wife greet each other with a kiss on the cheek.

c. _____ It is polite to make the *wai* to your grandmother.

d. _____ It is impolite to make the *wai* to your older cousin.

e. _____ Thai students look their teachers in the eye when they greet them.

f. _____ Businesswomen sometimes shake hands in Thailand.

g. _____ A male and a female cousin would shake hands in Turkey.

h. _____ The culture of Turkey is a mixture of European and Islamic culture.

i. _____ To greet someone close to your age, you would perform *el öpmek*.

j. _____ The forehead represents knowledge and respect in Islamic culture.

k. _____ Some older people expect this gesture from anyone younger.

Reflect on Reading

In Reading 2 you had to **infer** meaning. When you compared your answers with your classmates' answers, you probably found that you didn't always agree. **Inferences** are often not absolutely clear. They are inferences because the information is not clearly stated in the reading and you need to figure out the meaning.

3. *Check your answers in exercise 2 with a classmate.*

4. *Is* el öpmek *similar in any way to a gesture in Thailand? Explain why or why not.*

Adverbs give us more information about verbs, adjectives, and other adverbs. The underlined words below are adverbs of manner that tell *how* to do something.

To make this gesture, take the older person's right hand (palm side down) <u>lightly</u> in your right hand. Then kiss the back of the hand <u>gently</u> and place it against your own forehead.

5. *Complete the exercises below about adverbs.*

    a. Underline the five adverbs in these sentences from the reading.

Some people perform *el öpmek* routinely, that is, without really thinking about the meaning. For example, the older person may automatically move his or her hand to the younger person's forehead. This is not the best way to perform this greeting. If this gesture is made sincerely, it can be a deeply touching moment.

    b. What ending do most adverbs have? _____

6. *Circle the best word form choice in these sentences.*

    a. They usual/usually greet each other with a kiss on the cheek.
    b. The usual/usually way to greet each other is a handshake.
    c. He patted the child light/lightly on her head.
    d. It is always a light/lightly kiss, really just brushing your lips on the cheek.
    e. The gesture was very sincere/sincerely.
    f. When this gesture is made sincere/sincerely, it can be beautiful.
    g. His reaction to the smile was automatic/automatically.
    h. I automatic/automatically hugged him after so many years.
    i. It was a routine/routinely hug, with little meaning.
    j. They routine/routinely moved around the room, shaking hands with everyone at the party.

7. If you know common endings for different word forms, you can improve your reading skills. Complete the tasks that follow.

ANSWER KEY

   a. Find words in the reading on Turkish greetings to complete this chart.

Noun	Verb	Adjective
	greet	
extension		extended
connection		connected
knowledge	know	
interest	interest	
		respectful
		respected
appreciation		appreciated

   b. Give an example of a typical noun ending. _____

   c. List two typical adjective endings. _____ _____

....

Transitions help the reader understand the relationship between ideas in your writing.

1. Study the transitions on the next page.

Targeting

Transitions

For more information about transition expressions, see pages 217–218 in Reference.

Rules	Examples
Transitions usually go at the beginning of a sentence and are followed by a comma.	**First,** you put your hand up. **Second,** you move it back and forth. **Also,** you smile. **Finally,** you wave.
Also may go between the subject and verb or at the end of the sentence.	You **also** smile. You smile, **also.**
Phrases such as *the first* [noun], *the second* [noun], *the last* [noun] must have a verb following them when they are the subject of the sentence.	**The first step** *is* to put your hand up. **The last part** *is* hard to do.

2. Look at "Nonverbal Communication" on page 41 in Chapter 4. Find transition words or main points to complete this chart. The paragraph numbers are given for you.

Transitions	Main Points
Paragraph 1 (none) also The third way	facial gestures _____ _____
Paragraph 2 (none) _____ _____	instructions or warnings warmth negative feelings

3. *Complete this paragraph. Use appropriate transition words.*

We use three different greetings depending on the relationship to the person. _____*First*_____, we shake hands with a stranger. It doesn't matter if this person is male or female. _____, we kiss friends on both cheeks. We _____ kiss family members on both cheeks, but some people hug family members. The _____ greeting is for older people. We usually take their right hand into both our hands and hold it very gently.

··

Writing

Preparing to Write: Organizing Information

Spending time organizing your information before you write will make it easier for you to write in a clear, logical manner.

The author of *Trusty Travel Tips* wants to revise the book. She is adding information to the chapter on greeting gestures around the world. She needs your help with appropriate greetings from your culture.

Here are two common ways to organize your greetings.

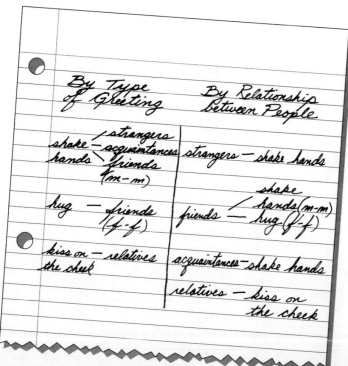

1. *Make a short list of items in two possible ways to organize your ideas.*

   by type of greeting   *by type of relationship*

   _____   _____

   _____   _____

   _____   _____

   _____   _____

   _____   _____

2. *Remember that you are writing for a book about traveling around the world. It is always important to **consider your audience.** Put a check next to the people who will be the readers of this guide. You may check more than one item.*

   _____ People who know you personally

   _____ People who don't know you

   _____ People who have been to your country

   _____ People who are interested in going to your country

Writers of travel guides keep their sentences impersonal. This means they use the third *person (he, she,* or *they).* They also may use the impersonal *you.* Travel guide writers usually do not include themselves (*I, me, my, mine*) in any descriptions.

3. *Which of the following descriptions are good examples of imper-sonal writing for a travel guide? Put a check (✓) on the lines.*

ANSWER KEY

a. _____ When I meet an older male relative, I bow to him. The older male will probably pat me on the back or shake hands with me.

b. _____ Korean students usually greet an older person or a teacher with a bow. They will never shake hands with a teacher or an older person.

c. _____ The *wai* is the most common greeting in my country, Thailand. To make the *wai,* I first put my hands together in front of my chest and bow my head slightly.

d. _____ When a woman meets a stranger, she turns her eyes away from the stranger. If she doesn't do that, the stranger will get a wrong impression.

4. *Find the descriptions that are too personal in exercise 3. Rewrite them so that they are more impersonal.*

ANSWER KEY

_____

_____

_____

_____

_____

_____

*Write a description of greetings in your culture for the book **Trusty Travel Tips.** Use the information from Preparing to Write on pages 51–52 to help you.*

Writing a Descriptive Article

WRITING TIP

Because you are writing for a travel guide, keep the sentences impersonal. Use the third person *(he, she,* or *they).*

Editing and Rewriting

Editing for Organization

One way to check your organization is to make a brief outline of what you have written. What are your main points? What are details or examples of your main points?

Editing Checklist

Check the Content

1. *Exchange your description of greetings with a classmate. After you read your classmate's description, answer these questions.*

   ❏ Are the parts of the description clearly organized?
   ❏ Is the description impersonal? Does the writer use third person words or the impersonal *you*?

Check the Details

2. *Now, reread your own writing. If necessary, revise what you wrote. Then continue checking your own writing. Use these questions.*

   ❏ Did you use the present tense for habits, general truths, or facts?
   ❏ Do the third person singular verbs have an -s or -es?

3. *Make your corrections and rewrite your description of greetings.*

Vocabulary Log

What words or phrases would you like to remember from this chapter? Write five to ten items in your notebook. Examples are on page 11.

Grammar and Punctuation Review

Look over your writing from this chapter. What changes did you need to make in grammar and punctuation? Write them in your notebook. Review them before the next writing assignment.

Class Activity   Detecting Lies

1 How good are you at reading the nonverbal communication of lying?

2 Take about five minutes to think of a true experience you have had or make up an experience. Tell your story to the class and let them vote on whether your story is true or false.

3 Keep statistics on how successful the class is in detecting lies.

Chapter 5

Gestures Around the World

Gestures have different meanings in different cultures. In this chapter you will write instructions on how to make a gesture from a culture of your choice.

Starting Point

Understanding Gestures

Do you know or can you guess what these gestures mean?

1. *With a classmate, look at these gestures and put a check (✓) next to all of the meanings that it has in your cultures. If you think of another meaning, write it on the last lines.*

Gestures	Meanings

a.

_____ the best   _____ the number 1

_____ OK   _____ the number 5

_____ (something   _____
         very insulting)   *(your idea)*

_____ hitchhiking   _____
                                  (your idea)

b.

_____ yes   _____ I don't know.

_____ no   _____
                                  (your idea)

Gestures	Meanings

c.

_____ victory   _____ the number 2

_____ peace   _____
                        (your idea)

_____ (something   _____
        very insulting) *(your idea)*

d.

_____ yes   _____ I am angry
                                with you.

_____ no   _____
                        (your idea)

_____ I agree with   _____
        you.   *(your idea)*

e.

_____ Goodbye.   _____ Come here.
                                (to an animal)

_____ Come here.   _____
                        (your idea)

f.

_____ (something   _____ Don't do that!
        very insulting)

_____ Goodbye.   _____ Go away!

_____ Hello.   _____
                        (your idea)

Gestures	Meanings	

g.

_____ We have   _____ Come here.
a secret.

_____ I like you.   _____
(your idea)

_____ I'm just joking.   _____
(your idea)

h.

_____ money   _____ I'm curious

_____ yes   _____
(your idea)

_____ I don't   _____
believe you.   (your idea)

2. *Complete these sentences about nonverbal communication.*

   a. In my country, **thumbs up** means _____.

   b. When you **move your head back and forth,** it means

   _____.

   c. If a man **winks** at another man, it means _____.

   d. If you **raise an eyebrow,** it means _____.

   e. If you **make a V with two fingers,** it means _____.

3. *In your culture, how do you communicate the following feelings or attitudes with body language? Discuss each with a classmate and show the gesture. Then answer the questions. Use the second person, **you**.*

a. What do you do if you want to call a waiter?

If you want to call a waiter, you raise your hand above

your head.

b. What do you do if something is delicious?

_____

c. What do you do if you want to show you are a good listener?

_____

d. What do you do if you are hungry?

_____

e. What do you do if something is expensive?

_____

f. What do you do if you are angry?

_____

g. What do you do if someone is crazy?

_____

h. What do you do if you don't understand?

_____

Targeting

....

Ways to Give Instructions

It is sometimes difficult to write instructions clearly. Using the correct verb forms is one way to make your instructions clear.

1. *Study these rules.*

Rules	*Examples*
To give instructions, use the *imperative,* the simple form of the verb.	**Keep** your head straight. **Don't look** the person in the eyes.
You may also use *should +* *verb*	You **should keep** your head straight. You **shouldn't shake** hands too long.
Use *you* and *your* in the instructions.	**You** should raise **your** head.

2. *Use these words to complete the instructions for making the gesture described in "The Salute" below. You may use them more than once.*

your   you   should   keep   be

The Salute

To make this gesture, raise ___*your*___ hand to the side of

_____ eyebrow. You _____ keep your fingers together.

Your arm should _____ parallel to your shoulder and to the

ground. _____ the palm of _____ hand up and forward at a

slope of 45 degrees. _____ your eyes on the flag until the flag

has been raised. When you make this gesture, _____ should

stand up with your chin up and _____ chest out. In Taiwan, this

gesture means respect for your country.

....

Thinking of each step in a process helps you to write clear instructions.

1. *Read this example of instructions. After reading it, can you make the gesture?*

An American Wave

To make this gesture, first raise your hand a little above your head. It should be at least twelve inches to the side of your face and six inches forward. Next, put the palm of the hand out. Keep the wrist stiff. Finally, make a motion from left to right. You should try to use the whole forearm and hand. Do this at least three times. This gesture means "good-bye."

2. *Underline all of the parts of the body in this reading above. How many are there? Next, underline all the transition words.*

Writing

Preparing to Write: Information in Instructions

3. *You are going to write a similar description of a gesture. Complete these steps to prepare to write.*

   a. Name a gesture. _____

   b. Define the gesture.
   This gesture means _____

   _____.

   c. List the parts of the body necessary to do the gesture.

   _____   _____   _____

   d. List the steps to make this gesture. Describing in detail each individual step in the process will make your instructions clearer.

   _____

   _____

   _____

   _____

   _____

   _____

   _____

   _____

   _____

Writing Instructions

Write instructions for a gesture. Follow the model in Preparing to Write.

> **WRITING TIP**
>
> Use **transitions** to make the steps in the process clear to your reader.

Editing and Rewriting

Read your description to a classmate. Ask your classmate to demonstrate the gesture. Can he or she make the gesture correctly? If not, decide what information is missing from your description.

Reading Your Work Aloud

EDITING TIP

When you read your writing aloud, you or your classmates may find mistakes in your writing.

Editing Checklist

Check the Content

1. *Exchange your instructions with a classmate. After you read your classmate's instructions, answer these questions.*

   ❏ Are the steps clear and in logical order?
   ❏ Are there enough transition words to make the order clear?
   ❏ Is the description impersonal?

Check the Details

2. *Now, reread your own instructions. If necessary, revise what you wrote. Then continue checking your own writing. Use these questions.*

   ❏ Did you use imperatives and *should* in the steps in your instructions?
   ❏ Did you use the present tense for facts, habits, and general truths?

3. *Make your corrections and rewrite your instructions.*

Vocabulary Log

What words or phrases would you like to remember from this chapter? Write five to ten items in your notebook. Examples are on page 11.

Grammar and Punctuation Review

Look over your writing from this chapter. What changes did you need to make in grammar and punctuation? Write them in your notebook. Review them before the next writing assignment.

Chapter 6

Comfort Zones

In this chapter you will read about "comfort zones" in different cultures and study ways to present data in a chart.

Starting Point

Finding a Good Distance

How close do you stand next to someone to feel comfortable? What is your "comfort zone"? This activity will help you find out.

1. *Stand about three feet from a classmate. Is this a comfortable distance for talking to him or her? Now move in (move closer) about a foot. Is this a comfortable distance for talking? Finally, stand toe-to-toe. Is this amount of space comfortable for you?*

2. *What information did you find out in exercise 1 above? Record the information in the chart. Write **OK, too close,** or **too far apart.** The first one has been suggested for you.*

Reaction of You and Your Classmate to These Distances for Talking			
	3 Feet Apart	2 Feet Apart	Toe to Toe
you	*too far apart*		
your classmate			

3. *Imagine your classmate is a close friend. Would you touch his or her arm while you talk? Is this a comfortable gesture for you?*

Reading

Comfort Zones

This reading explains comfort zones in different cultures.

1. *Read the following selection.*

Comfort Zones

[1] How close to another person do you like to stand? In our private lives, we usually stand close to friends and family. In public, an American usually stands two or three feet away from the other person. In some Latin American countries and in the Middle East, the distance is much less—people stand almost toe to toe. Different cultures have a different sense of how close to stand. For that reason, if a Mexican stands too close to an American, the American feels uncomfortable. In fact, the American usually backs away to keep a more comfortable distance. In contrast, if an American stands too far away, a Middle Easterner may feel uncomfortable. In Asian countries, the distance that people stand apart is much farther than in the United States. Two Chinese speakers will stand more than three feet apart.

[2] The amount of touching you do while you talk is also part of comfort zones. Touching someone's arm, hand, or back is okay in some cultures but not okay in others. Ken Cooper watched people talking in outdoor cafes in different countries. He then counted the number of touches of self or the other person in one hour. The results were San Juan, Puerto Rico, 180 times; Paris, 100 times; Florida, 2 times; and London, 0 times. In general, people in these places do not touch:

Japan, the United States, Canada, England, Scandinavia, northern European countries, Australia, and Estonia. The "touch countries" are the Middle Eastern countries, Latin American countries, Italy, Greece, Spain, Portugal, some Asian countries, and Russia. Four countries are in the middle: France, China, Ireland, and India.

[3] One comfort zone that seems to be universal is the distance people stand from each other in an elevator. The elevator is a good place to look at comfort zones. If one or two people are on the elevator, they will stand against the walls. If there are four people, each

stands in a corner. However, when five or six people get on, everyone faces the door. They try very hard not to touch each other. People look at the numbers on the floor indicator or they look down at the floor. They never turn and look at the strangers in the elevator. If they do this, the other passengers usually feel uncomfortable.

Taking notes with charts, diagrams, and pictures can help you review information quickly when you study.

2. *Complete these **diagrams** as **reading notes**.*

    a. *What are comfortable distances in different cultures between two people talking? List the countries on the lines. The X's represent the distance between the people.*

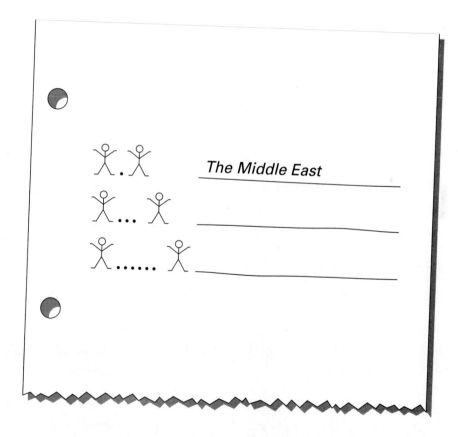

The Middle East _____

_____

_____

b. *Write the touch and non-touch countries in columns.*

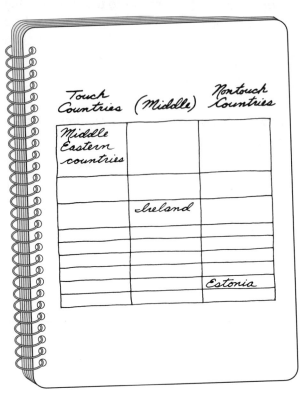

Touch Countries	(Middle)	Nontouch Countries
Middle Eastern countries		
	Ireland	
		Estonia

c. *Mark the distances of people in elevators. The **X's** represent the distance between the people. The boxes represent elevators.*

2 people   4 people   6 people

☐   ☐   ☐

3. *Put a **T** in the blank if the sentence is true. Put an **F** in the blank if the sentence is false. Read "Comfort Zones" again, if necessary.*

ANSWER KEY

a. _____ Cubans probably touch more in conversations than Australians do.

b. _____ In conversations, Portuguese touch more than Japanese.

c. _____ While talking, people in Ireland touch less often than people in England.

d. _____ If there are four people on an elevator, they will look at the ceiling.

e. _____ If you look at strangers in the elevator, they will feel uncomfortable.

f. _____ In Ken Cooper's study, Parisians touched less often than Puerto Ricans.

Reflect on Reading

Discuss these questions with a partner or a small group.
When you take notes, do you use words only or do you also use diagrams, charts, and illustrations? In which of these situations would illustrating ideas graphically be important?

Reading the newspaper   Reading a textbook for a course   Reading a story

Writing

Preparing to Write: Formatting Charts

As students and in your work life, you will sometimes need to present information in chart form. Later in this section, you will create your own chart. The following exercises will help you make your chart clear and easy to read.

1. *When you show information in charts, you want it to be complete but also easy to read. To make your chart very clear, try to use these features.*

- highlighted headings (for example, **bold,** <u>underline</u>, or *italics*)
- abbreviations
- a key to explain abbreviations

- shading
- darker grid lines
- different size letters
- different colors (especially if you are making the chart by hand)

The following charts show these different features.

2. *The information in Charts A, B, and C shows when touching is polite in different cultures. Four countries are included: Argentina, Russia, Saudi Arabia, and Thailand. With a partner, look at each chart, and decide what features help make the data difficult or easy to read. Take notes and then share your ideas with the whole class.*

   a. *What makes this chart difficult to read?*

Chart A

From	To	Arm	Hand	Shoulder	Back	Head
a child	an older person	Argentina, Russia	Argentina, Russia, Saudi Arabia	Argentina, Russia	Argentina	Argentina
a man	a woman	Argentina	Argentina, Thailand, Russia, Saudi Arabia	Argentina, Russia	Argentina	Argentina
a teacher	a student	Argentina, Thailand, Saudi Arabia	Argentina, Thailand, Russia, Saudi Arabia	Argentina, Thailand, Saudi Arabia	Argentina Thailand, Saudi Arabia	Argentina Thailand, Saudi Arabia

b. *Is this chart easier to read than Chart A? Why?*

Chart B

From	To	Arm	Hand	Shoulder	Back	Head
a child	an older person	Argentina, Russia	Argentina, Russia, Saudi Arabia	Argentina, Russia	Argentina	Argentina
a man	a woman	Argentina	Argentina, Thailand, Russia, Saudi Arabia	Argentina, Russia	Argentina	Argentina
a teacher	a student	Argentina, Thailand, Saudi Arabia	Argentina, Thailand, Russia, Saudi Arabia	Argentina, Thailand, Saudi Arabia	Argentina Thailand, Saudi Arabia	Argentina Thailand, Saudi Arabia

c. *Is this chart easier to read than Charts A and B? Why?*

Chart C

From	To	Arm	Hand	Shoulder	Back	Head
a child	**an older person**	A, R	A, R, SA	A, R	A	A
a man	**a woman**	A	A, T, R, SA	A, R	A	A
a teacher	**a student**	A, T, SA	A, T, R, SA	A, T, SA	A, T, SA	A, T, SA

Key: Argentina (A), Russia (R), Saudi Arabia (SA), Thailand (T)

d. *Do you think Chart D (on the next page) is easier or harder to read than Chart C? Why?*

Chart D

	A Child to an Older Person	A Man to a Woman	A Teacher to a Student
Argentina	arm, hand, shoulder, back, head	arm, hand, shoulder, back, head	arm, hand, shoulder, back, head
Russia	arm, hand, shoulder	hand, shoulder	hand
Thailand	—	hand	—
Saudi Arabia	hand	hand	arm, hand, shoulder, back, head

Writing

Writing Data Results in Charts

After you collect the data, you can choose how to present it in a chart. *Choose one of the following tasks. Work with a partner or a group to complete it.*

1. *Talk to people from different cultures. Ask them to stand at different distances from you. Then measure the comfort zones for public or private conversations. Ask them, "Do you feel comfortable at this distance?" Make a chart to show comfortable distances in different cultures for conversations.*
   or

2. *Talk to people from different cultures. Ask , "Is it okay to touch someone during a conversation?" If it is okay, ask, "What is it okay to touch—arm, hand, shoulder, back?" Are the rules different for a child, an older person, a man, a woman, a teacher? Make a chart to show when and where it's okay to touch for different cultures.*
   or

3. *Observe elevator behavior. Keep a record of how many people are in an elevator. Where do they stand? Where do they look? What happens if you look someone in the eye? Make a chart to illustrate the results of your elevator experiment.*

WRITING TIP

Always include a few introductory sentences to explain charts or graphs.

Consistent formatting means using the same form when you have items in a series or in a chart. Using consistent formatting makes your writing stronger and easier to read.

1. *Study these rules for consistent formatting in charts.*

Rules	Examples	
Use consistent formatting in charts or lists. Be consistent about these things:		
Capitalization	Bowing Shaking Hands *(capitalized words)*	bowing shaking hands *(lowercase words)*
Punctuation	Greeting: bow Distance: 2 feet *(colon)*	Greeting—bow Distance—2 feet *(dash)*
Grammar Structures	friend: 1 foot stranger: 2 feet *(singular topic words)*	friends: 1 foot strangers: 2 feet *(plural topic words)*

2. *Which chart has consistent formatting? Circle the letter.*

a.

distance talking to	a Friend	stranger
(in feet)	2	three

b.

distance talking to	a friend	a stranger
(in feet)	2	3

c.

distance talking to	a friend:	stranger
(in feet)	2 feet	3'

3. *Rewrite Chart A in Chart B. Make sure the capitalization, punctuation, and structure are correct and consistent.*

Chart A

number of People	2	four
position in Elevator	2 back corners	all four corners

Chart B

Editing Checklist

Check the Content

1. *Exchange your chart with a classmate. After you read your classmate's chart, answer these questions.*

   ❏ Above the chart, is there an introduction to the data?
   ❏ Is the chart complete and easy to read?

Check the Details

2. *Now, reread your chart. If necessary, revise what you wrote. Then continue checking your own writing. Use these questions.*

   ❏ Do you need to delete or shorten words?
   ❏ Would a key help?
   ❏ Do you need to highlight headings and separate them from data?
   ❏ Is there a better way to organize your data?
   ❏ Did you put all the data in parallel form—all nouns, for example?
   ❏ Is there consistent capitalization and punctuation?

3. *Make your corrections. Redo your chart if necessary.*

Vocabulary Log

What words or phrases would you like to remember from this chapter? Write five to ten items in your notebook. Examples are on page 11.

Grammar and Punctuation Review

Look over your writing from this chapter. What changes did you need to make in grammar and punctuation? Write them in your notebook. Review them before the next writing assignment.

③ Pets or Pests?

Millions of people around the world are pet owners. Some people love their pets and treat them almost like members of the family. However, not everyone thinks animals are a joy to live with. In this section, you will read and write about pet issues.

These are some of the activities you will do in this unit:

- Read descriptions of pets and problems with pets
- Read about pet therapy
- Write a letter of request
- Describe a pet or a pest
- Write a policy memo

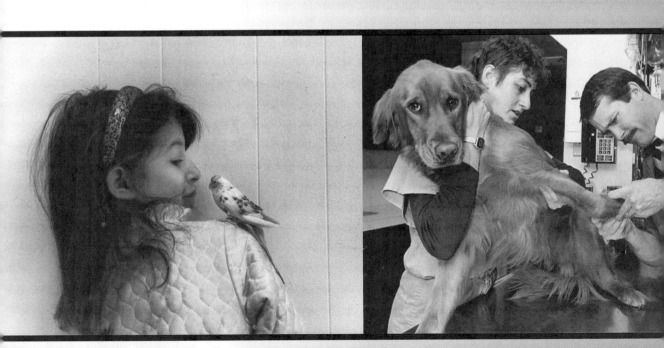

Chapter 7

The Great Debate

Do you love dogs, or do you think they're too noisy? Do you hate cats, or do you let them sleep on your bed? Would you prefer to have an iguana for a pet? People love to argue about pets. In this chapter you will read about and discuss pet preferences. You'll also have a chance to explain your feelings about pets.

Starting Point

Pet Preferences

Does your family have house pets? Are they common in your culture? In the United States, house pets are very popular.

1. *Nearly 53 million homes in the United States have pets. But which pets are the most popular? Make a guess. Number your choices from 1 to 6 for the most popular pets in the United States.*

   _____   reptiles

   _____   cats

   _____   birds

   _____   dogs

   _____   fish

   _____   small animals such as rabbits, hamsters, and gerbils

   See page 87 for the answers.

2. *Which pet would you prefer? Are cats better pets than dogs? Is a dog really a human's best friend? Are birds smarter than cats? Do fish help people relax? With a classmate or in small groups, discuss the advantages and disadvantages of these pets. Complete the chart on the next page. One suggestion has been made for you.*

	Advantages	Disadvantages
dogs		
cats	independent	
fish		
birds		
other: _____		

3. *Compare your chart with other charts in the class.*

Reading

....

Lorenzo the Loro Sometimes pets become part of the family. This reading selection talks about one family pet that made a big impression.

1. *Read the following selection.*

Lorenzo the Loro

[1] Recently, my Colombian host family visited me in the States, and the first thing they said was, "Greetings from Lorenzo!" It warmed my heart because for twenty years Lorenzo, the Loro, has remained a strong memory of a romance during my year in South America. I can

still see him standing on his perch in the kitchen, a royal parrot, green with a yellow forehead. *Loro* is Spanish for "parrot," but Lorenzo didn't limit himself to Spanish or bird talk. He was a parrot of the world.

[2] When I knew him, he was only ten years old, but what a talker! He spoke German to the German shepherds, meowed to the cats, and quacked to the ducks, "Quack, quack, quack, what pretty ducks!" When the doorbell rang, he said, "Who is it?" He sang along with the songs on the radio—one word behind. He talked only to the women in the house, so everyone was sure he was a male. He loved to eat scrambled eggs, and when it rained, the family put his perch outside where he happily took a shower. He didn't need a cage because he didn't try to fly away. He was happy on his perch in the kitchen, the hub of human and animal activity in the house.

[3] One day, when I arrived at the house, I asked my usual question, "How is Lorenzo today?" My host family said, "He is in a very bad mood; he hasn't spoken to anyone all day." I went into the kitchen and found him on his perch, turned around facing the wall, his back to me. "Lorenzo, do you want some chocolate? Do you want some chocolate?" He turned around and came close to my face and we laughed and we laughed. "Ha, ha, ha!" he said, "What a laugh! What a laugh!" That's when I knew we had something special between us and that I was in love.

2. *Match the topic of the paragraph with the paragraph number. Write the letter on the line.*

a. a special memory
b. an introduction to the pet
c. usual activities

_____ paragraph 1

_____ paragraph 2

_____ paragraph 3

3. *Read "Lorenzo the Loro" again for details.* **Infer** *which of the following are true. Write* **T** *for true and* **F** *for false on the lines.*

   a. _____ The writer is male.

   b. _____ Lorenzo spoke only in Spanish.

   c. _____ Lorenzo's family had other pets.

   d. _____ The family kept Lorenzo in a cage in the kitchen.

   e. _____ The writer lived in Colombia for ten years.

   f. _____ Sometimes Lorenzo was moody.

   g. _____ Lorenzo liked to eat chocolate and scrambled eggs.

   h. _____ The writer fell in love while living in Colombia.

4. *Circle all of the adjectives or adjective phrases that best describe Lorenzo.*

humorous	uninteresting	talkative with men
colorful	bored with life	international
unintelligent	musical	capable of feelings
moody	unhappy with his	
intelligent	family	

Targeting

....

Adjectives

There are many adjectives in the reading and exercises about Lorenzo. Adjectives describe nouns. You can often recognize an adjective by its suffix, or ending. Some common endings are *-ous, -ful, -able, -y, -ent, -al, -ing, -ed,* and *-ive.*

Decide if the following sentences need the adjective or noun form shown in each pair. Write the word in the blank.

   colorful, color

1. He was a very _____ bird with bright red, green, and yellow feathers.

2. His head was the _____ of grass in early spring.

humorous, humor

3. He had a great sense of _____. He made us all laugh.

4. He told another _____ story of his cat, who loved to eat popcorn.

moody, mood

5. They weren't in the _____ to play. They were too tired.

6. I wouldn't call him a _____ person. He was just a very quiet person.

talkative, talk

7. When you mentioned horses, my grandmother became

very _____. She had grown up riding at an early age.

8. The _____ was about the high cost of pet care in this country.

musical, music

9. She wanted a canary because they are very _____ birds.

10. Loud rock _____ upsets the cats, but they

love classical _____, especially Mozart.

romantic, romance

11. The time they spent together was very _____.

12. It is hard to imagine a _____ with a bird.

impressionable, impression

13. My host family's pets have left a big _____ on me. When I go back to Japan, I would like to own a cat.

14. Because the boys were young, they were very _____.

For more information about adjectives, see Comparatives and Superlatives on page 212 in Reference.

Quickwriting

Pets and You

How do you feel about pets? Do you think you could ever fall in love with a bird? Write for five or ten minutes in your notebook about your attitude toward pets.

Writing

Preparing to Write: Providing Supporting Ideas

Your writing will be stronger and more interesting if you provide concrete support for your ideas. You can use a variety of supporting techniques in your writing.

1. *Study these common types of support. The main idea in each example is underlined.*

Type of Support	Examples
1. stories, examples, specific details	One time, our parrot got me into a lot of trouble. My dad said I had to stay home all weekend. I disobeyed him and went out without telling him. When I came in quietly late in the night, the parrot loudly called out my name! My dad woke up and saw me coming in. I was grounded for two weeks after that.
2. facts, statistics, information from an authority	Because of advances in medicine, pets are living longer than they used to. Cats may live from sixteen to twenty years. Small dogs may live up to sixteen years, and large ones, eleven.
3. reasons, causes, and effects	When I was a child, I was chased by a large dog. It was a terrifying experience. I can still hear the pounding of his paws and his growling. I thought he was going to eat me alive! Therefore, dogs have always frightened me, and I have never wanted to own one.

2. *Look at the examples below. What kind of support do they use? Underline the main idea, and identify the kind of support technique used. Give the number of the type of support from the chart on page 82. Some items may use more than one kind of support.*

a. _____1_____ <u>Lorenzo was a real talker!</u> He spoke German to the German shepherds; he meowed to the cats. He quacked to the ducks, "Quack, quack, quack, what pretty ducks!" When the doorbell rang, he said, "Who is it?" He sang along with the songs on the radio—one word behind.

b. _____ A random survey of ESL students in our program regarding their pet preferences showed that dogs are the most popular pet. Sixty percent of the students liked dogs, and forty-eight percent had actually had a dog at some time in their lives. The most popular type of dog was the German shepherd. Many students described this dog as the most faithful and enjoyable to own.

c. _____ Cats are more interesting than dogs. First of all, cats are independent. They only come to your lap if they want to. They are not like dogs, who are always jumping up on you and demanding attention. Cats don't tie you down. You can go away for a week without worrying about them. Second, cats are cleaner. They keep their bodies clean, and they don't smell bad like dogs. Also, unlike dogs, they cover up their messes in the yard.

d. _____ My dog Salsaree was a very fierce dog. He always barked at people, even if they visited our home often. If a stranger touched his head, Salsaree would fly at the person.

e. _____ I think Americans try to extend their pets' lives too long with expensive medical treatments. Dr. Ana Bouvilla, who directs the Animal Disease Center in Florida, says that owners should think about whether it is really fair to keep their pet alive even when it has a serious disease.

f. _____ Dogs are very intelligent. When my dog, Jo Jo, was hit by a car, I frantically searched for him, but he was nowhere to be found. I called our local animal hospital to tell them that Jo Jo had been injured and that I was going to bring him in if I could ever find him. To my surprise, the nurse said, "He just checked himself in!" Apparently, after the accident, Jo Jo had walked about a mile from our house to the animal hospital. That's where he usually stays when the family is out of town.

g. _____ According to the documentary _Our Feathered Friends,_ without love and companionship, parrots will become mentally ill, and no amount of love can cure them. Sometimes they are simply neglected by their owners, who lose interest in them. These people don't realize that buying a parrot is like adopting a child. Also, because parrots can live very long lives, they may outlive the families that raised them, and, as elderly birds, they may be left in the hands of strangers. If you buy a parrot, you are making a long-term investment in pet care.

Writing with Supportive Ideas

Choose one of the following topics to write about.

1. Write a description of your favorite pet. Include details and anecdotes so the reader will like this pet, too. Use "Lorenzo the Loro," on pages 78–79, as a model.
2. What are some negative aspects of owning a pet? Give details and examples to support your opinions.
3. What animals make the best pets and why?

Editing and Rewriting

··

Editing for Sentence Completeness

Sometimes it is difficult to decide if a sentence is complete or not.

1. _Study the following rules about sentences._

Rule	Incorrect	Correct
A complete sentence has a *subject* and a *verb.*	They better animals.	They **are** better animals.
Words like *that, who,* and *because* can connect two ideas.	**Because** they are good pets. (This is incomplete because it has only one idea, and you need another main idea with *because*.)	**I prefer cats** because they are good pets. *or* Because cats are good pets, **we always have one around the house.**
	The dogs **that he owns.** (The main idea is missing.)	The dogs **that he owns are very gentle.**
Two complete sentences can-not be connected by a comma. Separate them into two sentences or connect them with a conjunction, a transition word, or a semicolon.	My mom liked cats, my dad hated them.	My mom liked cats. My dad hated them. My mom liked cats, **but** my dad hated them. **Although** my mom liked cats, my dad hated them. My mom liked cats; my dad hated them.

2. *Find the errors in sentence completeness. Correct them.*

   a. I dislike dogs because very smelly.

   b. Dogs are faithful, cats are unfaithful.

   c. A small white kitten who was covered with ashes from the fireplace.

   d. They always noisy and try to jump on me when I go to visit.

e. Because we aren't home enough to take care of a pet.

f. When I meet new dogs, I always careful to have them smell my hand before I pet them.

g. Because in my house my mother was always worried about cleanliness.

h. Dogs love to play with sticks. For example, fetch a stick if you throw it.

i. If you don't talk to your bird.

j. The dog that we used to have very friendly.

Editing Checklist

Check the Content

1. *Exchange your writing about pets with a classmate. After you read what your classmate wrote, answer the question.*

   ❏ Is there enough support for the ideas?

Check the Details

2. *Reread your own writing. If necessary, revise what you wrote. Find places to add specific details, facts, reasons, examples, or anecdotes. Then continue checking your own writing. Use these questions.*

   ❏ Did you use descriptive verbs?
   ❏ Are habits, truths, or facts in the simple present?
   ❏ Check the verb tenses. Do they show the right time (past or present)?
   ❏ Are your sentences complete?
   ❏ Look for commas. Do they connect two sentences? If they do, use a conjunction, or make two sentences.

3. *Make your corrections and rewrite your composition.*

Vocabulary Log

What words or phrases would you like to remember from this chapter? Write five to ten items in your notebook. Examples are on page 11.

Grammar and Punctuation Review

Look over your writing from this chapter. What changes did you need to make in grammar and punctuation? Write them in your notebook. Review them before the next writing assignment.

Here are the answers to the pet ownership ranking exercise on page 77.

1. cats

2. dogs

3. fish

4. birds

5. small animals

6. reptiles

Class Activity Survey

1 Do a survey of the pet preferences of students in your school.

2 Make a chart of the results.

3 What conclusions can you draw? For example, are women generally cat lovers and men generally dog lovers? Do women prefer larger or smaller animals than men do? Do people from different countries prefer one animal over another? Which breeds are the most popular?

Chapter 8

Pet Therapy

If you're lonely or sick, a pet can cheer you up and make you feel better. Many elderly people, especially, take great comfort from a loved dog or cat. In this chapter you will read an announcement about pet therapy and write a letter of request.

Starting Point

Doctor Pet?

Some people believe that pets can be therapeutic; that is, they can help people get well or feel better.

Discuss this question with a partner or a small group.

Do you think that a pet can help people feel better or get well? Explain your answer.

Pets are making the news with their ability to help hospital patients and the elderly.

RABBITS HELP MENTALLY ILL PATIENTS GAIN SELF-CONTROL

Therapy Pets Uplift The Depressed

Rooster Effective in Animal-Assisted Therapy Program

Visiting Animals Cheer Up Hospital Patients

Animals Have Calming Effect on Mental Patients

PETS CUT DOWN NUMBER OF SUICIDES

1. *Read the following selection.*

The Healing Power of Pets

[1] Many researchers are finding that the most serious disease for older people is not cancer or heart disease: It's loneliness. In fact, people die of broken hearts. Love is the most important medicine we have, and pets are one of nature's best sources of love.

[2] Dogs and cats help everyone overcome loneliness because they give companionship and affection. Pets can make you laugh and take your mind away from your troubles. They can also help you make more friends, and they encourage good health through exercise. Studies show that pets help us to relax, be healthy, and live longer. If you suffer from heart disease or stress, a hug a day may keep the doctor away. But if hugs are hard to find, the next best thing may be a dog or a cat in the lap. For an older person whose wife or husband has died, a pet may be the only being that he or she can touch and

talk to. A pet can help us cope with the loss of a loved one and help us adjust to a change in a living situation.

[3] Many elderly and lonely individuals have discovered that pets satisfy their needs and keep them in the world of deep emotional relationships. Having a pet to care for gives them a sense of self-worth. According to a study in the *International Journal of Aging and Human Development,* many elderly Americans think having a pet is more important than moving to a convenient place to live where pets are not allowed.

[4] Patients in hospitals or nursing homes who have regular visits from pets are more eager to get well. Visiting pets lift the spirits of residents. The elderly begin to care about the world around them again. Talking to pets has a health benefit, too. When people talk to people, blood pressure tends to go up, but when people talk to pets, blood pressure remains lower. In one study, depressed patients who did not want to work to regain lost skills were given pets to play with. The pet therapy worked. The patients began to smile and cooperate with the doctors. A pet is always there and eager to please, no matter what the person's condition.

(ANSWER KEY)

2. *The author describes many **cause-effect relationships** in the reading. Some relationships are stated directly. Some you will need to **infer.** Complete the chart to show these relationships.*

a.	*Loneliness can result in*	dying of a broken heart.
b.		can cure loneliness.
c.		keep the doctor away.
d.	If you have pets as a topic of conversation,	
e.		their blood pressure does not go up.
f.	When patients' spirits are higher,	
g.	When depressed patients were given pets to play with,	

3. *List the health benefits of owning a pet.*

Physical Health

Mental Health

_____   _____

_____   _____

_____   _____

_____   _____

_____   _____

(ANSWER KEY)

4. *Apply the information you learned in the reading. With a classmate, match the specific examples in the left column to the positive aspects of pets in the right column. Write the number on the line.*

(ANSWER KEY)

a. _____ Cats love to be petted. They will sit on your lap and you can stroke their fur.

b. _____ I know what my dog will do. There are no surprises. When I come home from work, he will jump up and down with his leash in his mouth. He'll want to take a walk.

c. _____ After we left home and my parents were alone, they bought a cocker spaniel and loved it so much that it was like a member of the family.

d. _____ I enjoy watching a tank full of fish. The marine life is silent, yet in motion. I completely forget about all my problems.

1. Pets are a substitute for children.

2. Pets provide a sense of home and family.

3. Pets provide security.

4. Pets provide physical contact.

5. Pets are predictable.

6. Pets are relaxing to be with.

7. Pets are fun.

8. Pets provide intimacy without the need for a conversation.

e. _____ Our bird loves to hang upside-down in her cage. It always makes us laugh.

f. _____ I can spend hours doing my schoolwork with my yellow cat on the couch beside me. We don't talk, but I feel very close to him.

g. _____ Our dog barks any time a stranger comes on our property.

h. _____ Our cats are part of our lives from the moment they come in for breakfast until we put them out at night. Their routines are part of our day.

Reflect on Reading

If you understand what you read, you should be able to use the information in different situations. This is called **applying information.** You did this in exercise 4 when you applied information you learned in the reading. This skill involves **critical thinking**—analyzing information or situations.

In which of these situations would you need to apply information from your reading?

Reading a telephone book   Reading a textbook   Reading the directions for changing a tire

5. *Find words in "The Healing Power of Pets" to complete the missing word forms in the chart below.*

ANSWER KEY

Noun	Verb	Adjective	Adverb
discovery			
convenience			conveniently
satisfaction		satisfactory	satisfactorily
(person)	to research		
		lonely	
		affectionate	affectionately
			internationally
depression	to depress		
cooperation		cooperative	cooperatively
	to develop	developmental	developmentally

6. *Complete this paragraph with the correct word endings, where necessary.*

ANSWER KEY

Pet therapy is a relatively new develop_____ in psychiatry,
(a)
but more and more research_____ are interested in the use
(b)
of animals in treating the sick and the elderly. We don't know for

certain when this idea began or who discover_____ it. The
(c)
first recorded use of animals to help patients was in a psychiatric

hospital in York, England, in 1972. Patients had responsibility for

the care of rabbits and chickens.

Since then, pet therapy has become internation_____
(d)
because it is a satisfactor_____ and convenien_____ way to
(e)   (f)

treat all ages and types of patients. Perhaps the greatest

benefit is that pets want affect_____. They break down the
                                   (g)

walls of lone_____ because they make patients want to
                (h)

socialize. Patients who are very depress_____ begin to smile
                                             (i)

and cooperat_____ with doctors. That willingness to get
             (j)

better makes all the difference in the world.

Writing

....

Preparing to Write: Adding Specific Details

The next writing assignment is a response to a notice in the news-paper. Providing enough details is very important in this response. (See Chapter 7, Preparing to Write, page 82 for more information about adding details.)

1. *Read the notice and answer the questions.*

San Antonio Times, December 12, 1997

Loving Pets Wanted as *Visiting Pets*

Do you have a loving pet to share with the elderly, the sick, and the lonely? Your pet could make a difference in someone's life. If you think your pet would make a good Visiting Therapist, write to:

Visiting Pet Program
P.O. Box 5489
San Antonio, TX 78231

   a. Why did the Visiting Pet Program put this notice in the news-paper?

   b. What is this organization looking for?

Some people have already replied to the Visiting Pet Program notice. However, they have not included enough details for support in their letters.

2. *Read the following letter to the Visiting Pet Program. With a classmate, underline the parts of the letter where the author needs to add more details. Then write questions that will encourage more information.*

Dear Visiting Pet Program:

I read about your program in the newspaper. I am interested in it. I think my cat would be a good Visiting Pet. He's very friendly.

I hope that you will accept him. I look forward to hearing from you.

Sincerely,

Marcy Yi

Marcy Yi

Which newspaper? What date? _____

_____

_____

_____

_____

_____

_____

3. *Look at the details in this letter. Do they answer all of your questions? If not, add more details.*

Dear Visiting Pet Program:

I read about your Visiting Pet Program in the *San Antonio Times*, December 12, 1997. I am very interested in your program. I think my cat, Dasher, would be a good visiting pet.

Dasher's a very cute, yellow, short-haired cat with a loving pesonality. Although he is only two years old, he does not run around very much. When strangers come to our house, he goes in and out of their legs and tries to get on their laps. I think an older person would be very happy with him. He loves to be petted.

I would like to participate in this pet therapy program, so I hope that you will accept him. I look forward to hearing from you.

Sincerely,

Marcy Yi

Marcy Yi

Imagine you have the perfect pet for the Visiting Pet Program and that you want to answer the call for volunteers by writing to the organization.

4. *To prepare to write, complete these sentences.*

    a. I read about your therapist pets in _____.

    b. I am interested in your _____,
        which was advertised in the December 12 issue of the *San Antonio Times*.

5. *Match these beginnings of sentences (column A) with logical conclusions (column B). Write the correct letter on the line.*

ANSWER KEY

A	**B**
_____ I am writing to tell	**a.** to become a visiting pet.
_____ I would like my cat	**b.** a very good visiting pet.
_____ I would very much like	**c.** you about my very loving pet.
_____ My cat would be	**d.** my cat to be in your program.

6. *Giving specific information helps the reader understand your writing. (To review giving specific information, see Chapter 7, Preparing to Write, page 82) Put a check (✓) next to the sentence in each pair that gives more information.*

ANSWER KEY

    a. _____ I would like my pet to be in your program.

           _____ I would like my turtle to be in your program.

    b. _____ My cat would be very good in your Visiting Pet Program.

           _____ My cat would be very good in your program.

    c. _____ I would very much like my dog to be in your program.

           _____ I would very much like my German shepherd to be in your program.

    d. _____ I am writing to tell you about my pet guinea pig.

           _____ I am writing to tell you about my very affectionate pet guinea pig.

7. *Complete these sentences with appropriate information.*

a. My cat would be a good visiting pet because _____

_____.

b. My bird is very friendly to strangers. For example, _____

_____.

c. My dog has a lot of experience with _____

_____.

d. My pet rat is good with _____

_____.

e. If my pet turtle visits people, he will make _____

feel _____.

8. *Imagine that you are a relative of someone who is in a nursing home or hospital where the management is considering using pet therapy. What are some of the potential problems of having animals in these environments? With a classmate, brainstorm and write a list of concerns that you have about this kind of program. Then share your list with the class.*

_____

_____

_____

_____

_____

_____

_____

9. *What information do you need from the Visiting Pet Program so that you will feel less worried about having animals in the nursing home or hospital?*

_____

_____

_____

_____

_____

_____

_____

_____

_____

Writing a Letter of Request

What do you think of the idea of pet therapy? Write a letter of request to the Visiting Pet Program in San Antonio. Use a separate piece of paper.

a. *Express your interest in the program and request that they consider your pet for a Visiting Pet. (You can use your imagination here!)*

or

b. *Express your concerns about this kind of program and ask for specific information about the potential problems that trouble you.*

Because your letter should be formal, use business letter format. The form on the next page is block style. You may use it as a model or use it to write a draft of your letter. Remember to single-space paragraphs in a formal letter.

For information about other letter formats, see Reference pages 210–211.

date	_____
your name and address	_____ _____ _____
Visiting Pet Program address	_____ _____ _____
greeting	_____:
how you heard about the program	_____ _____
request to have your pet in the program and reasons that your pet is a good choice OR expression of concerns and a request for more information	_____ _____ _____ _____ _____ _____ _____ _____ _____
closing sentences	I hope that _____. I look forward to hearing from you.
closing	Sincerely,
your signature	
your name	_____

Editing and Rewriting

Editing for Errors in Present Perfect Tense

1. *Study the rules on the following page.*

Rules	Examples
Use the present perfect tense for events that happened in the past and are continuing now or may happen again.	I **have** always **loved** dogs. (I have in the past and I will continue to do so.) Our cat **has** just **had** kittens. (It happened close to now.) We **have owned** several cats, but we **have** never **had** any dogs. (We had cats before and we will probably have them again. We may have dogs someday.)
The present perfect is commonly used with time expressions that explain *how long, how much,* or that show the relationship to the present.	We have had this puppy **for two weeks.** We have had a cat **since August.** **So far,** our cat hasn't paid too much attention to the puppy. They haven't gotten into any fights **yet**.
The simple past is used for events that were completed in the past. There is no expectation that they will happen again. If there is a past time phrase or clause, you cannot use the present perfect.	**When I was a child,** we always **had** cats. Our cat **had** a litter of seven kittens **last year.** I **raised** gerbils **when I was ten years old.**
When you edit for verb tenses, check whether you have changed tenses unnecessarily.	My roommate likes to rescue lost animals. I ~~hated~~ hate this, because I ~~have always been~~ am allergic to animals. (Use all present tense verbs.)

2. *Find the verb tense errors in these sentences and correct them. Some sentences have no errors.*

(a) My mom's cat loves chocolate. (b) Whenever she has ~~had~~ chocolate ice cream, he goes nuts until he can have some. (c) The cat has opened the kitchen door a couple of weeks ago because he had to get to the chocolate.

(d) My son is trying to raise two frogs from frog eggs. (e) So far, they were easy to take care of, but every week we have had to buy live crickets for them to eat. (f) Dinnertime was wild! It's fun to watch frogs, though.

(g) I have always been afraid of large dogs. (h) One has knocked me over when I was a child. (i) I still don't like them.

(j) Our cockatiel has known when my husband turns into our street. (k) He begins to squawk wildly until my husband has come in.

Editing Checklist

Check the Content

1. *Exchange your letter with a classmate's. After you read your classmate's letter, answer these questions.*

   ❑ Did the writer include a clear reason for writing?
   ❑ Are there enough details?

Check the Details

2. *Now, reread your letter. If necessary, revise what you wrote. Then continue checking your own writing. Use these questions.*

   ❑ If you used block style, are paragraphs lined up on the left?
   ❑ Are the paragraphs single-spaced?
   ❑ Did you use the present tense for general truths about your pets?
   ❑ Did you use the present perfect tense for events that happened in the past but are not finished or that may happen again?

3. *Make your corrections and rewrite your letter on a separate paper.*

Vocabulary Log

What words or phrases would you like to remember from this chapter? Write five to ten items in your notebook. Examples are on page 11.

Grammar and Punctuation Review

Look over your writing from this chapter. What changes did you need to make in grammar and punctuation? Write them in your notebook. Review them before the next writing assignment.

Chapter 9

Pet Peeves

Have you ever been annoyed by a neighbor's barking dog? Does your neighbor's cat come to your door to beg for food? In this chapter you will read complaints about pets and write an apartment pet policy memo.

Starting Point

Annoying Pets

People are often annoyed with other people's pets. This can frequently happen where people live especially close together, for example, in apartment buildings.

What are some typical problems that pets in apartments cause for non-pet owners? Discuss with a partner or a small group.

Reading

Your Pet Is Bothering Me

When people live close together, pets often bother neighbors. This selection lists common complaints that apartment owners have.

1. *With a classmate, **scan** these pet complaints. What is the animal? What is the problem?*

READING TIP

You don't always have to read every word. When you just need specific information, **scan** to find that information quickly.

Your Pet Is Bothering Me

a. "I live on the ground floor and have a lovely patio garden. Unfortunately, my neighbor has a small dog that loves to dig in my flower containers and make a mess on my small plot of grass. I can't take it anymore. The law says owners have to pick up after their dogs."

b. "This is the second time I've had to spray for fleas in six weeks. I am sick and tired of cats roaming in and out of my apartment. When I came back from the swimming pool yesterday, I found one curled up on my bed! Animals belong outside—not in people's homes!"

c. "Their parrot squawks from sunrise to sunset. I can stand the occasional noise of Saturday night parties up there, but that bird is driving me crazy. I can't stand the noise."

d. "This is just too much. Every time I walk down the hall, I have to cover my nose. The smell of those guinea pigs is terrible! I don't know if she doesn't keep the cage clean or if it's just the way those animals are."

e. "It's not that I'm against exotic pets. But I don't like to be in the laundry room with a snake. Why can't my neighbor clean his clothes without bringing that snake along? I don't care if it's not poisonous. It's creepy. If it's not around his neck, it's coiled up in his basket. It's making me nuts."

f. "I'm allergic to cats. I love this apartment, but it's a nightmare in hot weather when I have to open the windows. The neighbor's long-haired cat crawls out on the balcony, and I start sneezing and scratching."

g. "I realize that that dog is protecting us, but the barking is too much. It wakes me every night. I can't get enough sleep!"

Reflect on Reading

In exercise 1 you scanned for information. Often, there isn't enough time to read every word in a text. When you **scan,** you look for key words to quickly find what you need to know. Think of the kind of information you are looking for. If you need to find a date, look for numbers. If you need to find someone's name, look for capital letters.

2. *Make a list of the animals and the complaints that you remember from the reading. Don't look at the reading.*

(ANSWER KEY)

_____   _____

_____   _____

_____   _____

_____   _____

_____   _____

3. *Work with a classmate. Compare your list with a partner's. Now check the reading. How well did you scan the information? Did you remember all the situations?*

4. *Read "Your Pet Is Bothering Me" again, more closely this time. Now, find expressions that mean "something is upsetting."*

I can't take it anymore.   _____

_____   _____

_____   _____

_____   _____

_____   _____

_____   _____

5. *Complete these sentences with words and expressions from "Your Pet Is Bothering Me."*

a. A _____ is a paved outdoor space next to a house or building. People like to sit on it when the weather is nice. However, if you live in a second-floor apartment, you need a different structure for enjoying the outdoors. A _____ is an area that sticks out from the wall of a building. People in apartments often have these to sit out on in good weather.

b. _____ are tiny insects that are often on animals. They bite animals and humans. If they get indoors, they are hard to get rid of.

c. _____ are little ratlike animals that people keep in cages.

d. Snakes and other reptiles are examples of _____ pets. They are not common in households.

e. When a snake is in a circle, it is _____.

f. If you are sneezing and itching near an animal, you may be _____ to it.

For the next writing assignment, you need to organize information. There are a lot of different ways to do this. One way is to use a problem-solution approach.

You are the manager of the Blue Arms Apartments. This is a complex of five, six-story buildings, each containing thirty apartments. The ground-floor apartments have patios. The other apartments have balconies. The complex has common green areas and a swimming pool.

Recently, there have been a lot of problems at the Blue Arms Apartments because the pet policy is too loose. You are getting complaints about pets, and if you don't come up with a stricter policy, you are going to lose tenants.

1. *Work with a partner or in a group to complete the chart. List the problems the apartment complex is having. You may use problems from "Your Pet Is Bothering Me" on pages 104–105 or add pet problems that you know of. How could a new policy solve each problem? Write your ideas in the second column.*

Problems	New Policy
fleas on cats	All cats must have flea collars.

2. *Policy statements must be clear and to the point. Complete the following tasks to work on a policy statement.*

   a. *You are writing a pet policy memo. State the reasons for the policy in the first paragraph of the memo. You want to bring people over to your side by explaining the problem clearly. Complete this paragraph with reasons for a new pet policy.*

For several years we have had a very casual pet policy at the Blue Arms Apartments. However, in recent years

_____

_____

_____

_____

_____

_____

_____

_____

_____

As a result, we have adopted a stricter pet policy. We hope that this will eliminate the problems that we have been experiencing.

b. *In the second paragraph of the memo, be specific about each item of the policy. Underline the words in these statements that make the points of the policy specific:*

- Only two cats are allowed per apartment.

- Large dogs are allowed in ground-floor apartments only.

- Dogs and cats must wear flea collars at all times.

- Owners must keep their dogs on a leash at all times when outside the apartment.

c. *Use numbers or bullets to highlight the specific parts of the new policy. Study these examples.*

1. Only two cats are allowed per apartment.

2. Large dogs are allowed in ground-floor apartments only.

- Only two cats are allowed per apartment.

- Large dogs are allowed in ground-floor apartments only.

d. *What will happen if your tenants don't follow the new policy? In the last paragraph of the memo, be direct about the consequences, but also encourage cooperation.*

If this policy is not followed, we regret that _____
_____
_____
_____
_____
_____
_____
_____
_____
_____

We appreciate your cooperation in this matter.

Writing a Policy Memo

Memos are letters written for people who live or work in the same organization or place. They usually begin with this format:

To:

From:

Date:

Subject:

WRITING TIP

Single-space memos. Double-space between paragraphs. Do not indent.

Memos are written in **block style,** that is, without indenting of paragraphs. There is no closing or signature at the bottom of the memo.

Write a memo to the tenants of the Blue Arms Apartments. Explain the new pet policy.

It's important to make sure that singular count nouns are not bare. If they are, you have several ways to correct your mistakes.

Editing for Errors with Singular Count Nouns

1. *Study the rules about count nouns below.*

Rules	Examples
A *count noun* can never be bare or stand alone.	***Incorrect*** There are cat here. I have cat. It's cat. Where is cat? We gave cat a name.
A count noun must be "covered" by a plural ending or a determiner.	***Correct*** *Add a plural ending:* There are **cats** here.
A determiner gives *basic* information about a noun. Typical determiners are articles, possessives, demonstratives, and quantifiers.	*Add a determiner:* I have **a** cat. (*article*) It's **my** cat. (*possessive*) Where is **that** cat? (*demonstrative*) We gave **each** cat a name. (*quantifier*)
Adjectives give *extra* information about nouns, but they are not determiners.	***Incorrect:*** They are beautiful cat. ***Correct:*** They are beautiful cat**s**.

Rules	Examples
If you have a bare count noun in your writing, something is wrong. Ask yourself these questions. 1. What can I add to "cover" this noun? 2. Is the noun really plural? (Add a plural ending.) 3. If the noun is really singular, can I add a determiner? Which determiner?	**Incorrect** **Correct** We are friend. → We are friend**s**. I have friend. → I have **a** friend. He's friend. → He's **my** friend.

2. *Underline all of the count nouns in these paragraphs. Which ones are bare? How can you correct these errors? The first sentence has been done for you.*

(a) <u>People</u> are usually cat <u>lover</u>S or cat <u>haters</u>. (b) These animals bring out strong reaction in people. (c) Some famous cat hater were Adolph Hitler, Napoleon, Julius Caesar, and Mussolini. (d) President Dwight D. Eisenhower was serious cat hater. (e) He ordered people to shoot cat seen on property.

(f) Among cat lover is Islamic prophet Mohammed. (g) His cat, Muezza, once fell asleep on sleeve of robe. (h) When Mohammed was called to prayers, he didn't want to wake cat. (i) Instead, he cut off sleeve of robe. (j) Another cat lover was Winston Churchill. (k) He was very fond of cat, Jock. (l) He even took him to cabinet meeting during war. (m) Dr. Albert Schweitzer, Nobel Peace Prize winner, actually became ambidextrous (equally able to use both right and left hand) because of cat, Sizi. (n) Dr. Schweitzer normally used left hand. (o) However, when Sizi fell asleep on left arm, he forced himself to write with right hand.

Editing Checklist

Check the Content

1. *Exchange your memo with a classmate. After you read what your classmate wrote, answer these questions.*

   ❏ Can you understand the reasons for the pet policy?
   ❏ Is the policy clear?
   ❏ Is there a request at the end or a thank you for cooperation?

Check the Details

2. *Now, reread your memo. If necessary, revise what you wrote. Then continue checking your own writing. Use these questions.*

   ❏ Is your memo single-spaced?
   ❏ Is it double-spaced between paragraphs?
   ❏ Did you use bullets or numbers for the parts of the policy?
   ❏ Are any singular count nouns bare? If so, fix them.
   ❏ Did you use the past tense for events that happened in the past?
   ❏ Did you use the present perfect for events that happened in the past but are not complete or are still important now?
   ❏ Are all your sentences complete?

3. *Make your corrections and rewrite your memo.*

Vocabulary Log

What words or phrases would you like to remember from this chapter? Write five to ten items in your notebook. Examples are on page 11.

Grammar and Punctuation Review

Look over your writing from this chapter. What changes did you need to make in grammar and punctuation? Write them in your notebook. Review them before the next writing assignment.

Healthy Choices

What do you do to stay healthy? Exercise, diet, and lifestyle choices affect your health and the way you feel. In this unit you will read and write about ways to stay healthy.

These are some of the activities you will do in this unit:

- Read directions for getting started on a walking program
- Write guidelines for an activity
- Read about trends in cafeteria food
- Write a suggestion memo
- Read a description of the ecopsychology movement
- Read advice for simplifying your life
- Write an analysis of a lifestyle

Chapter 10

Walking

The cheapest form of exercise is also one of the simplest—walking. This chapter gives you practice in reading and writing about walking and other free-time activities.

....

Starting Point

Do you exercise to keep yourself in good physical shape?

Exercise Survey

1. *Complete this survey.*

On a scale of 1 to 5, how
important do you think
exercise is? Circle one number.
Here, *5* means "the most important."   1   2   3   4   5

On a scale of 1 to 5, how
hard is it for you to exercise
regularly? Circle one number.
Here, *5* means "the hardest."   1   2   3   4   5

Explain your answers.

_____

_____

_____

_____

How many times a week do you
exercise for more than twenty   1   2   3   4   5
minutes? Circle one number.   6   7   8   9   10

What kind(s) of exercise(s) do you do?

_____

_____

_____

2. *Share the information from the survey with a partner or a small group.*

3. *In your class, what are the three most common ways people exercise?*

Reading 1

Walks of Life

Many people walk for exercise. The following is from a magazine article about walking for exercise.

1. *Read the selection on the following page.*

Walks of Life

Want to sleep better, think better, learn better? Take a walk!

Just thirty minutes of walking per day can significantly improve your health. Most people know that regular walking can improve your physical health, but many don't know the other benefits of walking. It can also help you sleep better, learn better, and respond faster. It reduces depression and anxiety, lessens stress, boosts self-esteem, and increases energy.

Walking is also low-impact and easy to do. "After all," says Chuck Ways, an exercise physiologist, "we were designed to walk."

Getting going

Even though walking is so natural, Ways recommends starting out gradually, giving your body time to adjust. "If you've been inactive, walk just ten or fifteen minutes per day, and then slowly build up your time. Once you can regularly walk twenty minutes a day, then you can focus on distance."

Ways adds, "After you've built up some endurance, it's important that you don't stroll, but walk briskly." That means walking quickly enough to deepen your breathing and increase your heart rate. It also means you can carry on a conversation with someone while you walk— though with some difficulty.

Walking tips

Here are some tips for walking.
- *Shoes.* Comfortable, well-fitting shoes are a must. Be sure there's a thumbnail's width between the shoe end and your big toe. Look for good arch support and "breathable" uppers (see "Tips for Buying Walking Shoes" for other tips).
- *Technique.* Stand up straight; keep your head erect, your shoulders back, and your abdomen in. Land on the heel of your foot and roll forward onto the ball of your foot. Swing your arms as you walk.
- *Clothes.* Wear loose, comfortable clothes and dress for the weather. In the summer, wearing cotton clothes will help your body heat to escape. In colder weather, dress in warm layers.

Tips for Buying Walking Shoes

- Shop for shoes later in the day; feet tend to swell during the day.
- Have your feet measured while you're standing.
- Be sure to try on both shoes and to walk around the store (or outside, if they'll let you).
- Buy for the larger foot— both feet are rarely the same size.
- When trying on shoes, wear the kind of socks or stockings that you plan to wear with the new shoes.
- Don't rely on the shoe size of the last you bought. Feet get larger over the years.
- Shoes should be comfortable immediately—if someone tells you the shoes need a "break-in" period, don't buy them.

ANSWER KEY

2. *Find these things in the reading.*

    a. In the first sentence of paragraph 2, underline a word that the writer uses to make a connection to paragraph 1.

    b. In the first sentence of paragraph 3, the writer repeats an idea from paragraph 2. Underline the idea that is repeated (in different words) in both paragraphs.

    c. In the first sentence of paragraph 4, underline a word that the writer uses to make a connection to paragraph 3.

ANSWER KEY

3. *When you take notes from a reading, you often* **summarize** *the reading. Order these ideas from 1 to 5 to make a summary of "Walks of Life." Write the numbers on the lines.*

    a. _____ once walk twenty minutes a day, can walk a longer distance

    b. _____ when begin, start out gradually

    c. _____ also tips about buying shoes, walking correctly, and dressing appropriately

    d. _____ walking good because very beneficial—also easy to do

    e. _____ best to walk briskly but not so fast that can't carry on a conversation.

4. *Write your notes below. Include a short list of the advantages of walking given in the reading.*

Notes from "Walks of Life"

Benefits:

5. *Here are some things you can **infer** from "Tips for Buying Walking Shoes" in the box. Which tip is each related to? Write the letter of the inference next to the tip in the reading.*

- **a.** You should always have your feet measured.
- **b.** Some stores want you to buy shoes even if the shoes don't feel good on your feet.
- **c.** You shouldn't try your shoes on barefoot.
- **d.** Your foot is a different size when you are seated than when you are standing.
- **e.** If you buy shoes early in the morning, they may not be comfortable later in the day.
- **f.** You should always try on both shoes.

6. *Complete these sentences with one of the words in parentheses.*

- **a.** You may need to _____ the way you walk so

    that you _____ your chance of injury.
    (adjust, lessen)

- **b.** Sometimes people go through a period of _____.

    They often feel _____ during this period.
    (anxiety, depression)

- **c.** Walking helped me _____ my health.

    Every day I _____ the distance I walked.
    (improve(d), increase(d))

- **d.** We didn't notice how _____ we were improving our physical health because the change

    happened so _____.   (gradually, significantly)

- **e.** We _____ along and looked in all the shop windows. Then we realized that it was time to get on the

    ferry, so we _____ quickly down to the dock.
    (stroll(ed), walk(ed))

In exercises 2 and 3 you **summarized** the reading. In which of these reading situations would summarizing be important? How would it help you?

| Reading directions for a new product | Reading a textbook for a course | Reading a book about a famous person |

Summarizing is also an important writing skill. In which of these writing tasks would you need to summarize?

| Writing a description | Writing a research paper | Writing a report on a meeting |

Reading 2

One-Mile Walking Test

Walking is a great way to keep fit. Because of its low cost and its physical and mental benefits, it is now more popular than jogging or aerobics.

1. *Read the following selection.*

One-Mile Walking Test

Before you start a walking program, check your general fitness. Take the one-mile walking test.

1. For an exact distance, use a standard track or a measured and marked flat trail with a smooth surface. (A standard track is one-quarter mile, so walk four laps in the inside lane for the one-mile evaluation.) If you don't have a standard track, you should use a measured path, a street you have driven on to measure, or a treadmill.
2. Warm up for several minutes with easy walking and stretching.
3. Try to walk at a pace that's steady, but feels as if you're pushing hard. Remember, you'll probably walk at least ten to twelve minutes, so don't start too fast. If you feel strong in the last couple of minutes, pick up the pace.
4. Your goal is to feel tired, but not exhausted. You should feel slightly winded. If you are gasping and panting for air, you are pushing yourself too hard.
5. Cool down by walking slowly for a few minutes.
6. Check your time by using this chart to figure out your fitness level.

READING TIP

Don't worry if you don't understand every word. The first time through, focus on what you do understand. The second time through, look for **context clues** to the meanings of unfamiliar words.

Fitness Category	Minutes:Seconds for the One-Mile Test	
	Male	**Female**
high fitness	12:42 or under	13:42 or under
moderate fitness	12:42–15:38	13:42–16:40
low fitness	15:38	16:40

2. *Find the words in boldface in Reading 2. Underline them and try to guess their meaning from the* **context.** *Then match the beginnings of sentences in the first column with their appropriate endings in the second column. Write the numbers on the lines.*

ANSWER KEY

a. _____ A **measured** or **marked trail** is a trail

b. _____ **Stretching** means

c. _____ **Pace** is

d. _____ A pace that is **steady** means

e. _____ If you are **exhausted,**

f. _____ **Gasping or panting for air**

g. _____ A **lap** is

1. at the same speed.
2. one trip around a track.
3. means you are having trouble breathing.
4. making your muscles looser so that your body is warm enough to exercise.
5. how fast you walk.
6. you are very tired.
7. you know the length of.

3. *According to "One-Mile Walking Test," which of the following statements are true? Write* **T** *for true and* **F** *for false.*

ANSWER KEY

a. _____ It's impossible to figure out your own measured mile.

b. _____ Four laps equal one mile on a standard track.

c. _____ You should stretch your muscles before you begin walking.

d. _____ It's not a good idea to push yourself hard.

e. _____ You should not feel tired.

f. _____ Sit down immediately after finishing the mile.

Writing

Preparing to Write: Organizing Information

This section focuses on brainstorming ideas and outlining. These skills will help you prepare to write guidelines for starting a new activity.

1. _Work with a partner or a small group. Think of as many free-time activities as you can and write them in the list._

   walking _____   jogging _____   car racing _____

   flower arranging _____   _____   _____

   _____   _____   _____

   _____   _____   _____

   _____   _____   _____

2. _Compare your list with other students'. Choose one or two activities that you know something about._
3. _Study this brainstorming example._

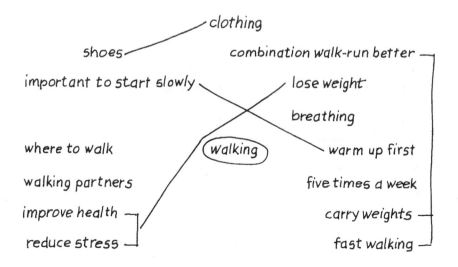

4. *Now, do your own brainstorming. Write one of the activities from exercise 1 inside the circle in the space below. Write any thoughts related to the activity outside of the circle. Draw lines to connect thoughts that are related. If you "get stuck" and can't think of any ideas, try starting again with a different activity.*

5. *Look again at "Walks of Life" on page 117. Which outline shows the way the article is organized? Circle the outline number.*

Outline 1	Outline 2	Outline 3
Topic: Walking	Topic: Walking	Topic: Walking

I.   Why this is a good activity
    A. [Add information about the topic.]
    B.
II. Things to consider when you start
    A.
    B.
III. Conclusion
    A.
    B.
	I. Introduction
	    A. [Add information about the topic.]
	    B.
	II. Why this is a good activity
	    A.
	    B.
	III. Things to consider when you start this activity
	    A.
	    B.
	IV. Helpful suggestions
	    A.
	    B.
		I. Introduction
		    A. [Add information about the topic.]
		    B.
		II. A description of how to do this activity
		    A.
		    B.
		III. Helpful suggestions
		    A.
		    B.

6. *Your next writing assignment is to recommend a new activity and make suggestions for how to get started doing it. Write a basic outline. Then fill in more information.*

Now, use the information in your outline to describe the activity and to give your recommendations and guidelines.

Writing About an Activity

Editing and Rewriting

Editing Real Conditional Sentences

Conditional sentences explain what happens or will happen under a certain condition.

1. *Study these rules.*

Rules	Examples
In a *real* condition, the *if*-clause is usually in the simple present tense.	If I **walk** every day, . . . If it **rains,** . . .
Do not use the future in the *if*-clause.	***Incorrect:*** If it **will rain** tomorrow, . . . ***Correct:*** If it **rains** tomorrow, . . .
When the *if*-clause begins the sentence, it is separated from the rest of the sentence by a comma (**,**).	If you **exercise** regularly, . . .
Sometimes you use other tenses or a modal in the *if*-clause.*the continuous action.*) If you **can walk** every day, . . . (*Your ability to walk every day is the condition.*)	If you **are walking** too fast, . . . (*The present continuous emphasizes*
The *result clause* can have a variety of verb forms, depending on the meaning.	If I walk every day, I **feel** healthy. (*general information*) If you walk a lot, you **will decrease** stress. (*future result*) If you are gasping for air, you **are pushing** yourself too hard. (*emphasizes the continuous action*) If you are pushing yourself too hard, you **may get** overly tired. (*possibility*) **Walk** every day if you want to stay healthy. (*command form*)

2. *Correct errors with verb tenses in the following real conditional sentences.*

ANSWER KEY

   a. You increase your lung capacity if you will walk.

   b. If you got more blood to the brain, you will think better.

   c. You can decrease your chance of getting heart disease or cancer if you walked.

   d. If you will walk with a friend, it will be more enjoyable.

   e. Your mood and energy level will improve even if you walked for only ten minutes.

3. *Complete the sentences with correct real conditional forms of these verbs.*

ANSWER KEY

be	increase	take
change	(not) become	walk
get	(not) get	wear

   a. If you _____*walk*_____, you ____*will increase*____ the strength of your heart.

   b. If you _____, you _____ more blood to the brain.

   c. If you _____ proper shoes, your feet _____ tired.

   d. If you _____ your route from time to time, you _____ bored.

   e. If you _____ facing the cars, you _____ safer.

   f. You _____ ready for all kinds of weather if you _____ a light rain jacket along.

Editing Checklist

Check the Content

1. *Exchange your writing about an activity with a classmate. After you read what your classmate wrote, answer these questions.*

   ❑ Is there an introduction to the topic?
   ❑ Do you understand the writer's main points? Is there enough information?
   ❑ Is the writer's organization of information clear?

Check the Details

2. *Now, reread your writing. If necessary, revise what you wrote. Then continue checking your own writing. Use these questions.*

   ❑ Did you connect ideas with transition words, with words that show additional information, or with repeated information?
   ❑ If you used a real condition, underline the *if* and result clauses. Are the verb tenses correct?
   ❑ Do all your subjects and verbs agree?
   ❑ Did you write complete sentences?

3. *Make your corrections and rewrite your information about the activity.*

Vocabulary Log

What words or phrases would you like to remember from this chapter? Write five to ten items in your notebook. Examples are on page 11.

Grammar and Punctuation Review

Look over your writing from this chapter. What changes did you need to make in grammar and punctuation? Write them in your notebook. Review them before the next writing assignment.

Chapter 11

What's on the Menu?

Typical institutional food can taste as good as homemade food or it can be bland and unappetizing. It also varies in quality and nutritional value. In this chapter you will look at a cafeteria menu, read about fat and disease, and write a memo that suggests changes to the food selection in the office cafeteria.

Starting Point

Looking at a Menu

Food we eat in cafeterias—typically at school, at work, or in hospitals—is called institutional food.

1. *Read the following cafeteria menu.*

MENU

Week	Monday	Tuesday	Wednesday	Thursday	Friday
9/9 to 9/13	hamburger and french fries	assorted meat sandwiches and potato chips	chicken salad and apple slices	bean tacos with rice	hot dog and potato salad
9/16 to 9/20	pepperoni pizza with tossed green salad	ham and cheese sandwich and cookie	steak with cooked carrots	chicken sandwich and fruit juice	spaghetti with meat balls

2. *A healthy diet is low in fat. Work with a classmate. Mark an **F** next to all the menu items that have a lot of fat and an **S** next to the ones that are high in salt.*

3. *A healthy diet has lots of fruits and vegetables each day. Put an asterisk (*) next to all of the fruits and vegetables on the menu.*

4. *Which day has the healthiest meal? _____*

Reading

Reduce Fat in Your Diet

What is the relationship between the amount of fat people eat and their health?

1. *Read about how to reduce your risk of disease by reducing fat in your diet.*

Reduce Fat in Your Diet

[1] The kind of food you eat is important. If you trim certain kinds of fat from your diet, you will help reduce your chances of serious disease. Reducing fat also helps you control your weight because fat contains more calories than proteins and carbohydrates do. Reduce fat, reduce calories, reduce weight. However, some fat is necessary to supply vitamins (A, D, E, and K) and energy. Dietary fat is also the only source of linoleic acid, which the body needs.

[2] Most of us, however, eat much more fat than our bodies need. Doctors recommend that we limit our intake of fat to no more than 30 to 35 percent of what we eat. For an average 1,500 calorie-a-day diet, that means about 50 grams or 3.5 tablespoons of fat or oil.

[3] The kind of fat you eat makes a difference, too. There is a relationship between saturated fats (found in meats, butter, cheeses, palm oil, and coconut oil) and cholesterol in the blood. Cholesterol is very important for the brain and nervous system. However, your body produces all the cholesterol that you need.

[4] When you add too much cholesterol to your blood, fatty deposits form in the arteries. These deposits make it difficult for the blood to flow. When the blood doesn't move well, serious problems can develop, such as arteriosclerosis (hardening of the arteries), heart disease, and strokes.

[5] Unsaturated or polyunsaturated fats, on the other hand, reduce cholesterol by helping the body get rid of it. These fats are found in vegetable or other plant oils such as corn, soybean, safflower, sunflower, or cottonseed oil, and in foods such as fish and walnuts.

2. If you **diagram** technical information, it will be easier to understand. Complete these diagrams with information from the reading.

ANSWER KEY

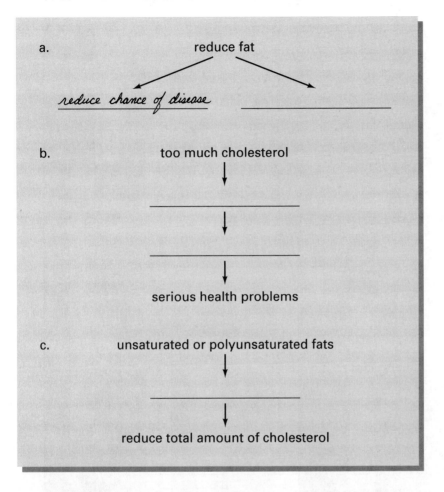

a.   reduce fat

   reduce chance of disease   _____

b.   too much cholesterol
                            ↓
                    _____
                            ↓
                    _____
                            ↓
                    serious health problems

c.   unsaturated or polyunsaturated fats
                            ↓
                    _____
                            ↓
                    reduce total amount of cholesterol

3. **Apply the information** in "Reduce Fat in Your Diet" to these choices. Put an **X** by the better of the two choices in each row.

ANSWER KEY

a. _____ baked chicken   _____ fried chicken

b. _____ fish   _____ red meat

c. _____ cheese   _____ vegetables

d. _____ sunflower oil   _____ butter

4. Complete the following crossword puzzle with the words from "Reduce Fat in Your Diet."

ANSWER KEY

- arteries
- arteriosclerosis
- deposits
- diet
- dietary
- fat
- food
- intake
- limit
- produce
- reduce
- rid
- trim
- weight

Across
1. your usual food and drink
4. get _____ of something you don't want
5. the material layer under the skin of humans
7. having to do with diet
8. fatty _____ are a result of too much cholesterol
11. hardening of the arteries

Down
2. what is allowed to enter
3. reduce
5. what we eat
6. blood vessels that carry blood from the heart to the rest of the body
9. make
10. how heavy you are
12. control the number or amount
13. lower

Writing

**Preparing to Write:
Evaluating with
Lists**

Listing items helps you look at your information and evaluate its usefulness before you write.

1. *Evaluate the food in the menu on page 127. Make two lists for the food choices, **healthy** and **unhealthy.***

    Healthy Food   **Unhealthy Food**

    _____   _____

    _____   _____

    _____   _____

    _____   _____

    _____   _____

    _____   _____

    _____   _____

    _____   _____

    _____   _____

2. *How does the food in your cafeteria or local restaurants compare to the food on the menu on page 127? Is it healthier? Is there a variety of food? In the appropriate column, list the positive and negative features of the menus in your cafeteria or local restaurants.*

    Positive Features   **Negative Features**

    _____   _____

    _____   _____

    _____   _____

_____   _____

_____   _____

_____   _____

_____   _____

_____   _____

_____   _____

Writing a Suggestion Memo

You are a member of a committee that has been studying the lunch menu at your office cafeteria. A sample of the two-week menu appears in Starting Point on page 127. As a group, you are very upset about the high-fat, boring lunches. You want to see low-fat meals, with more fruits and vegetables. You also want the menu to match the diverse cultural backgrounds of the people who work in the company.

Write a memo to the food service manager. Suggest ways to improve the lunches. Your memo should include the reasons for changing the menu and suggestions for the changes. (For tips on writing a memo, see Chapter 9, page 110.)

> **WRITING TIP**
>
> Use bullets (•) to high-light important items in a list in your memo.

Editing and Rewriting

Editing for Noncount Nouns

As you write about food, you may use some noncount nouns. They are often a problem in English.

1. *Study the following information about noncount nouns.*

Rules	Examples
Most nouns in English are *count* nouns. Count nouns can be singular or have a plural *-s* or *-es* ending. They can combine with plural expressions such as **many, several, ten.**	**a** hamburger, **three** carrots, **many** meals
Some nouns in English are *noncount* nouns.	fat, rice, juice, food
They are usually singular. Use mass expressions such as **much, a lot of,** or **less** to show quantity with noncount nouns.	**a lot of** food, **less** fat
Some nouns can be count and noncount, depending on the meaning.	Their **breakfasts** are very expensive. *(count because it refers to the breakfasts listed on the menu)* What's for **breakfast**? *(noncount because it refers to the activity)* How many **times** did you eat there? *(count because it means **occasions**)* How much **time** is there? *(noncount because it refers to the general category of time made up of smaller sections)* In my country there are many **fruits** that you can't find in the United States. *(count)* You should eat a lot of **fruit.** *(noncount)*

For information about the spelling of noun endings, see page 216 in Reference.

For more information about noncount nouns, see page 215 in Reference.

2. *Identify the noncount nouns. Put an* **N** *in the blank if the noun in boldface is a noncount noun.*

    a. Is there enough **rice** _____ for **dinner** _____?

    b. I'd like two **hot dogs** _____ with **French fries** _____.

    c. They ordered a pepperoni **pizza** _____ and a sausage pizza with **mushrooms** _____.

    d. We are out of **milk** _____. Could you pick some up at the **store** _____?

    e. A little **olive oil** _____ is healthier than **butter** _____.

    f. We need to make some more peanut butter **sandwiches** _____ for **lunch** _____.

    g. You can't make that sauce without a cup of brown **sugar** _____ and two tablespoons of **vinegar** _____.

    h. I didn't find any **information** _____ about dietary fat in that **magazine** _____.

    i. There wasn't a **definition** _____ of **cholesterol** _____ in that sentence.

3. *Study the information below about noncount nouns.*

Rules	Correct	Incorrect
Never use *a* or *an* with a noncount noun.	**milk** **spaghetti**	**a milk** **a spaghetti**
A noncount noun (with its noncount meaning) is singular.	lots of **rice** more **salt**, please	lots of **rices** more **salts**, please
Never use plural expressions with noncount nouns.	**a lot of** milk **less** flour	**many** milk **fewer** flours

4. *Identify the problems in these sentences. Some of the nouns and noun phrases are underlined. Correct any errors in their use. Some underlined words may be correct.*

ANSWER KEY

      Many
    ~~Much~~ company cafeterias are changing their menus. Workers
       (a)   (b)   (c)

today don't want many fat, and they know the health value of
                      (d)   (e)

fresh fruits and vegetables. They are used to variety. The standard
(f)   (g)   (h)

diet of meats and potatoes is not enough. People also want
         (i)   (j)

many international food. A good food means workers will return to
              (k)   (l)

their jobs with more energies to work. Lunchtimes should also be
(m) (n)   (o)

a mental break. The atmosphere of cafeterias is also changing.
      (p)   (q)

Good musics, tablecloths, fresh flowers, and even a colorful food
             (r)   (s)

help refresh the worker.

Because today's lifestyle is very busy, many workers do not have

times to cook dinner. For this reason some companies are offering
   (t)   (u)

healthy take-home dinner. This allows workers to spend more time
         (v)   (w)

with their families. They arrive home early without doing

grocery shoppings and don't have to cook.
       (x)

Editing Checklist

Check the Content

1. *Exchange your memo with a classmate. After you read what your classmate wrote, answer these questions:*

   ❑ Does the writer give reasons for the suggestions or decisions?
   ❑ Are the suggestions or decisions in a bulleted or numbered list?
   ❑ Is there a closing statement or comment?

Check the Details

2. *Now, reread you memo. If necessary, revise what you wrote. Then continue checking your own writing. Use these questions.*

   ❑ Did you use noncount nouns correctly?
   ❑ Did you use the present, past, and present perfect tenses correctly?
   ❑ Are your sentences complete?

3. *Make your corrections and rewrite your memo.*

Vocabulary Log

What words or phrases would you like to remember from this chapter? Write five to ten items in your notebook. Examples are on page 11.

Grammar and Punctuation Review

Look over your writing from this chapter. What changes did you need to make in grammar and punctuation? Write them in your notebook. Review them before the next writing assignment.

Chapter 12

Back to Nature

Do you notice the seasons, listen to bird songs, walk in the rain, enjoy the ocean or the mountains? Nature and the environment affect us in many ways. This chapter features an article about a new branch of psychology that studies this connection. It also gives advice on living simpler lives. After you read these articles, you will write an analysis of a lifestyle.

Starting Point

Ecopsychology

Ecopsychology is a new area of psychology. Ecopsychologists study humans and their relationships to the environment (*eco*). They feel that the environment is very important to our happiness.

1. *Work with a classmate. Put a check (✓) next to all of the activities on the following page that show a good relationship between humans and the environment.*

_____ walking on the beach   _____ visiting nature centers

_____ taking tree seedlings   _____ building more
       from a national park   skyscrapers

_____ hiking in the woods   _____ putting seeds out for
                                          wild birds

2. *Compare your answers with your classmates'.*

Reading 1

···

The Nature Connection

READING TIP

If you understand how a writer is **organizing information,** it can help you understand the writer's main ideas.

This selection explains the basic ideas ecopsychologists have about people and the environment.

1. *Read the following selection.*

The Nature Connection

[1] Ecopsychology is a new area of psychology. Ecopsychologists study humans and their relationships to the environment (*eco*). They feel that the environment is very important to our sense of well-being. In fact, they believe it is central to our happiness. If we are going to be happy, we need to connect more with nature. Children are born with this feeling of connection to nature. They often spend long periods of time with plants, trees, and insects. However, as we age, we often lose that sense of joy in nature.

[2] Over the centuries, we have become more isolated and disconnected from nature. This has hurt society. It has made us more violent, anxious, depressed, and lonely. People who are close to nature and have good relationships with animals have respect for life. They also have a better chance of being mentally healthy adults. When we understand our bond to nature—plants and animals—we will live together better as a society.

[3] Being a society that is separate from nature has also hurt the environment too. Vast areas of our natural world are disappearing. We are overdeveloping the earth and using its resources in an irresponsible way. It's time to stop this destructive pattern. Therefore, rather than spending our days in concrete buildings and around asphalt streets, we need to spend more time with nature. Activities such as sailing, gardening, mountain climbing, walking along a trail, or just relaxing in the backyard can help us reconnect with the natural world.

2. *What are the main ideas of the paragraphs? Write the paragraph numbers next to the appropriate titles.*

(ANSWER KEY)

_____ Harm to the   _____ Environment   _____ Harm to our
        environment   and happiness   mental health

3. *Circle the best answer.*

(ANSWER KEY)

  a. According to paragraph 1, which of the following statements is *not* true?

    1. It takes children a long time to get connected with nature.

    2. Ecopsychologists believe humans need a good relationship with nature.

    3. If we are closer to nature, we will be happier.

    4. As we get older, we are less connected with nature.

  b. According to ecopsychologists, being disconnected from nature causes _____ .

    1. respect for life

    2. good relationships with animals

    3. loneliness

    4. a bond to plants and animals

  c. Ecopsychologists believe that if we are connected with nature, we will _____ .

    1. spend more time downtown

    2. stop the destruction of nature

    3. separate ourselves from the natural world

    4. spend more time on leisure activities

4. *Match the words on the left with words on the right that are similar in meaning. Write the numbers on the lines.*

(ANSWER KEY)

  a. _____ well-being   **1.** connection

  b. _____ isolated   **2.** divided

  c. _____ separated   **3.** happiness

  d. _____ bond   **4.** kept apart from others

Reflect on Reading

Here are some typical ways to organize paragraphs. Which technique(s) best describe(s) the paragraphs in "The Nature Connection"?

a. one topic with facts or examples to support it

b. steps in a process or sequence; a list of points in chronological (time) order or in order of importance

c. a focus on the reasons and/or the results

d. a focus on similarities and/or differences

5. *Learning common prefixes and roots in English helps you understand the meanings of unfamiliar words more quickly. What do these prefixes mean? Complete the chart. Match the prefix with its meaning in the list and think of another word that has this prefix. (Note: One meaning is used for two prefixes.)*

again	environment	not
beyond what is necessary	in	together, with

Prefix	Meaning	Example from "The Nature Connection"	Another Example
eco-		ecopsychology	
en-		environment	
co-		connected	
dis-		disconnected	
over-		overdeveloping	
ir-		irresponsible	
re-		reconnect	

6. *Here are some common word roots. Find an example of a word with this root in "The Nature Connection." Then think of another word that contains this root.*

Root	Meaning	Example from Reading	Another Example
psych	mind		
velop	wrap		
struct	build		
nat	born		

How close are you to nature? Are you as close to nature as you were as a child? Write in your notebook for ten minutes about the importance of nature in your life.

**Quickwriting:
Your Nature
Connection**

Reading 2

There is a lot of talk today about how busy our lives are and the need for simplicity.

1. *Read what Cecile Andrews says about slowing down and about what it can do for our lives.*

**Slow Down, Slow
Down, Slow Down**

Slow Down, Slow Down, Slow Down

To live mindfully and to appreciate your time, you have to move slowly. There's nothing more difficult for us, and we have gotten worse at this in the last twenty years.

Court reporters find that we talk faster than we did twenty years ago. We also walk faster and our movies are faster. MTV is the perfect example. Just as we start to focus on an image, the camera moves on to another image.

What is this addiction to stimulation? Sometimes I feel addicted to my own adrenaline. If I'm not rushing or feeling pressured, I feel like I'm missing something.

Is this the only way we can feel alive now—by rushing? Are we mistaking the rush of caffeine for a feeling of vitality? Does rushing make us feel as if we are doing something important or that we are important people? Are we all doing such meaningless work that we can feel important only if we feel pressured? Do we have to convince ourselves and others of the importance of our work in order to justify our existence?

Here is where mindfulness comes in. You must pay attention to your speed and consciously slow down.

Rushing as we do means that things are always going wrong. We always drop things, break something, and have to clean up, so it takes longer to do the thing anyway. It's like speeding and getting stopped by the police: We lose all the time we were trying to gain.

And of course, in our rushing, we have no time to talk with people, so we get lonelier and lonelier.

In rushing, we have no time for reflecting and no time to notice what is going on around us. We can't reflect on warning signals that come to us—warning signals such as early signs that something is wrong with our health. We may miss signs that we are starting to drive too fast. For instance, whenever I have a near-miss accident in my car, I always say to myself, "Ahhh, a message from the universe." Then, I slow down and become more careful in my driving.

Once I walked in on a man who was robbing my house. On my walk up to the door, I had noticed several little things I later realized should have told me what was happening. But I ignored them. I escaped unharmed, but once again I thought to myself, "You ignored the signs. You didn't pay attention."

When we rush, we are much more likely to consume because we are ignoring the little voice inside that asks us if we really need this new thing. Impulse buying is what corporations depend on.

I think that little voice is always there speaking to us, telling us the right thing to do, but we ignore it because we are rushing and have no time to listen.

This is what I would like to feel more than anything—gratitude. How else can you really enjoy your life? To feel gratitude is to look at everything in your life and appreciate it, be aware of it, and pay attention to it.

Our lifestyle, of course, causes discontent and resentment. Because more is always better, we can never be satisfied with what we have. Because commericals are constantly showing us ecstatically happy people with lots of stuff, we always feel that we're just not quite making it. Then, when we see how much money rich people have, we feel envious.

All of these feelings make us discontent with our life, causing us to fail to be grateful for what we do have.

So, each morning, I consciously think about what I am grateful for and repeat e. e. cummings' words to myself.

i thank You God for most this amazing day: for the leaping greenly spirits of trees and a blue true dream of sky; and for everything which is natural which is infinite which is yes

2. *Number the paragraphs then, answer these questions about "Slow Down, Slow Down, Slow Down."*

a. What is Andrews's main point about how to live well?

_____

b. What makes Americans feel really alive?

_____

c. In paragraph 5, what do you think *mindfulness* means?

_____

d. Paragraphs 6 through 10 give four possible results of rushing. List them here.

_____

_____

_____

_____

e. What is one of the things the author thinks it is important to do?

_____

f. What does *gratitude* mean, according to the author?

_____

g. How does our lifestyle affect our sense of gratitude?

_____

h. Why does the author repeat e. e. cummings's poem every morning?

_____

i. e. e. cummings is a poet. Poets often ignore rules of writing. Find one example of this in one of the lines from his poem in the reading.

_____

Targeting

....

Collocations

Collocations are words that commonly go together in a language. Which preposition follows *spend time*? Is *start* followed by *to* plus the base verb or by the *-ing* form of the verb? Unfortunately, there is no easy way to know collocations. You must study them and try to use them correctly.

1. *Read these expressions. Notice the words and verb forms that appear together.*

Expressions	Examples
spend time + verb + *-ing*	You should **spend time** sit**ting** quietly.
waste time + verb + *-ing*	Don't **waste time** watch**ing** TV.
spend time with (something)	**Spend time with** a book.
spend time with (someone)	**Spend time with** a friend.
start to + verb	**Start to understand** the problem.
start + verb + *-ing*	**Start understanding** the problem.
stop to + verb (if it means start an activity after quitting another one)	He **stopped to say** "Hello."
stop + verb + *-ing* (if it means to quit doing something)	He **stopped spending** so much time there.
pay attention to (someone)	He never **paid attention to** her.
pay attention to (something)	Always **pay attention to** the conversation.
take the time to + verb	**Take the time to** listen to music.
rather than + verb	**Rather than stay home,** let's go hiking.
rather than + verb + *-ing*	**Rather than staying** home, let's go hiking.

2. Complete these sentences with ideas of your own about slowing down the pace of your life.

   a. Spend more time _____.

   b. Don't forget to pay attention to _____.

   c. It's a good idea to spend time with _____.

   d. Take the time to _____.

   e. I shouldn't waste time _____.

3. Correct the errors in the collocations in these sentences. Some sentences may be correct.

ANSWER KEY

   -ing
   a. Start think ∧ about ways to help the environment.

   b. He started climb mountains to be closer to nature.

   c. We need to stop to destroy nature.

   d. I have started to thinking about our next hike.

   e. We stopped to refill our water bottles.

   f. He usually wastes time to look for things he has lost.

Writing

Preparing to Write: Analyzing Information

The writing assignment in this unit is to analyze a lifestyle. These exercises will help you think of some ideas and decide what details to include.

1. _Before you write an analysis of a lifestyle, you need to assess what that lifestyle is. Fill in the following charts with ideas about your lifestyle or the lifestyle of someone else you know, and about the lifestyle of a group of people—for example, people in your country._

Lifestyle of an Individual	Pace of Life	Relationship to Nature
now		
in the past		

Lifestyle of a Group	Pace of Life	Relationship to Nature
now		
in the past		

2. *Look at your notes in the charts in exercise 1. Which do you have the most information about—your lifestyle or a whole group's lifestyle? Expand on these ideas. On a separate piece of paper, use the mapping technique for brainstorming that you saw in Chapter 10 on page 122.*

3. *Here are four examples of lifestyle analyses from students' papers. What aspects of lifestyle did each of these students decide to focus on? Put checks (✓) in the chart. You may check more than one aspect for each example.*

	a	b	c	d
analyzes an individual's lifestyle				
analyzes a group's lifestyle				
describes the present				
describes the past				
describes the pace of life				
describes the relationship to nature				

a.   When I was a university student in Korea, I think I was one of the busiest people in the world. Every day I had a lot of homework, and I had to clean the house, cook, wash the dishes, and talk on the telephone. I had to hurry to finish everything in a day. I was too busy with these tasks to think of other things. At that time, I often lost things. I couldn't remember where I had put them, and then I had to spend a lot of time searching for them. This forgetfulness was a red signal. It was a warning that I needed to stop doing so many things and slow down.

     Another problem I had was concentration. I was doing so many things that I couldn't keep my mind on one thing. When I was reading books, I couldn't concentrate on them. I had to stop reading, get up, and do something else, such as turn off a light or prepare my book bag for the next day of school. I wasted time doing unimportant things, yet I felt busy. This was not a pleasant feeling for me.

When you feel busy, you need to stop what you are doing and be still. You should ask yourself, "Is this really important? Is it necessary?" Every morning when you wake up, you should be aware of the day, and every night you should spend some time reflecting on yourself. If you have enough time to consider and think about your life, you will find out whether you are living a good lifestyle.

b.   To speak of the Thai lifestyle in present-day Thailand essentially means to speak of either urban or rural life, but most Thai people live in the countryside in a village setting. Most villages are on large areas of land near a river. A home is usually a simple wooden house raised above the ground on posts. Domestic animals such as water buffaloes, pigs, and chickens are kept below the house.

The rural areas of the provinces in Thailand have no sky-scrapers and traffic jams, so life seems very simple. Every day the inhabitants follow the same routine. They wake up, go to work, and then come back to have dinner at home. People spend most of their time with their families, friends, and neighbors. They always help each other if someone faces a problem.

Another aspect of their lifestyle is their belief in the power of nature. They get their food by hunting or farming. They even worship some types of trees, such as the *Ton Ta Kien Tong*. Because they have learned to live well with nature since childhood, some rural people are even able to survive in the jungle for several days. Childhood is a carefree time. Children are often seen roaming freely throughout the vil-lage. They play with anything close to nature, fly kites, plow imaginary fields, and hunt insects and harmless reptiles.

Thai life is close to nature from birth until death. This closeness has two faces. The good side is that nature helps people to be happier and healthier. The bad side is that a lot of rural people do not know how important nature is for them; therefore, they are allowing a lot of forest destruction. This is becoming a very serious problem. I hope that in the future, the forest destruction will decrease and that the Thai countryside will remain full of trees and wild animals.

c. My lifestyle has changed very much since I came to this country. When I lived in Saudi Arabia, I was busy, but it was a wonderful time. I liked the pace of my life. I spent a lot of time with my family. I have three brothers and one sister. Every Friday we had a big dinner with the whole family together. Then I would go out in the evening to visit friends. We would play cards, watch TV together, or go to nightclubs.

Now my lifestyle is so solitary and simplified that it is boring. I have so much free time that I get very lonely. I spend my time doing my homework or watching TV—that's all. I have so much homework that I only get about six hours of sleep a night, and that makes me irritable. I'm too young to go to nightclubs in this country, so I miss that.

In conclusion, I miss my past lifestyle a lot because I was much more active than I am now. I try to exercise a couple of hours at a gym each day because that helps my attitude. Most of all, I just try to keep in mind that this is a temporary lifestyle. I will eventually go back home.

d. When I was a primary school student, I was a boy scout. I learned how to live outdoors, and I had a lot of opportunities to camp. Every summer vacation, I went to the beach or to a valley. Because I liked to swim, I usually went to places near water. My favorite place was Hyunree. It has very clear water and beautiful scenery. When I went there last summer, I swam and fished by day. Every night, I made my meal and played the guitar by my campfire. It was the happiest time for me, an escape from the pollution of Seoul.

This summer I can't go to Hyunree because I am in the United States. But I have made a plan to travel to California to visit the national parks and the beautiful beaches. This will give me the many gifts of nature. When I finish this trip, I know I will feel that I am a man who is connected to nature again.

Writing an Analysis

When you write an analysis of a lifestyle, you describe and try to explain a way of living. The lifestyle you analyze may be yours or someone else's, or it may be the lifestyle of a whole group of people. You may focus on the idea of simplifying life and/or on the ideas of people's relationships with the environment.

Your analysis should give details. If you feel the pace of the lifestyle is okay, give details to prove it. If you feel the pace is not healthy, include some suggestions for improving it.

Write an analysis of a lifestyle. For ideas, reread "The Nature Connection" on page 138" or "Slow Down, Slow Down, Slow Down" on page 142. Begin with a general statement about the lifestyle.

Editing and Rewriting

Editing Checklist

Check the Content

1. *Exchange your lifestyle analysis with a classmate. After you read what your class-mate wrote, answer these questions.*

   ❏ Are the problems and suggestions clear?
   ❏ Is the writer's opinion supported with details?

Check the Details

2. *Now, reread your lifestyle analysis. If necessary, revise what you wrote. Add some information or reasons. Then continue checking your own writing. Use these questions.*

   ❏ Did you use the present, past, and present perfect tenses correctly?
   ❏ Have you used the common collocations on page 144 correctly? Pay special attention to phrases with *time.*
   ❏ Are your sentences complete?

3. *Make your corrections and rewrite your analysis.*

Vocabulary Log

What words or phrases would you like to remember from this chapter? Write five to ten items in your notebook. Examples are on page 11.

Grammar and Punctuation Review

Look over your writing from this chapter. What changes did you need to make in grammar and punctuation? Write them in your notebook. Review them before the next writing assignment.

Class Activity   Project Lifestyle

Keep a log of what you do for two weeks to improve your physical exercise, food intake, closeness to nature, or lifestyle. After two weeks, collect information from all the students and report your information in a chart.

or

Work together to plan a class session to encourage awareness of nature and of our need to be more connected with nature. Some possibilities are doing hands-on activities, taking a field trip, listening to a guest speaker, making presentations, or preparing a special food. Invite another class to participate in or to watch your special class session.

5 Celebrate!

People everywhere enjoy festivities and celebrations.

Here are some of the activities you will do as you go through this unit:

- Read about a festival in Thailand
- Learn vocabulary for describing celebrations
- Write a description of a celebration
- Read about special-interest days
- Write a summary
- Read and write a formal thank-you letter

Chapter 13

Festivities

In this chapter, you will identify holidays you know, read a description of a festival in Thailand, and write about a celebration that you know.

Starting Point

People have lots of different and interesting reasons for celebrating around the world.

Identifying Holidays

1. *With a classmate, discuss what is happening in each picture. Then match each picture with the appropriate holiday by writing the correct number on the line.*

1. **1.** Korean First Birthday Celebration, *Tol Chanch'i*

2. **2.** Japanese Coming of Age Day, *(Seijin-shiki)*, January 15

3. **3.** Turkish Republic Day *(Cumhuriyet Bayrami)*, October 29

4. **4.** Colombian Holy Week *(Semana Santa)*, Spring

a. _____

b. _____

c. _____   **d.** _____

2. *Put a check (✓) by things you celebrate in your family or culture. Then add any other celebrations to the list.*

_____ Girls' Day

_____ Boys' Day

_____ the death of a famous person

_____ the death of ancestors

_____ a birthday

_____ an engagement or a wedding

_____ a historical event

_____ a religious event

_____ the birth of a child

_____ the end or beginning of a period, such as fasting

_____ the completion of school

Other celebrations:

_____   _____

_____   _____

_____   _____

For more information about holidays, see page 213 in Reference.

3. *Survey your classmates to get the names, dates (if possible), and reasons for five celebrations from their families or cultures. If necessary, use some of the information about celebrations in Starting Point, page 153. Write your information in the chart on the next page.*

Holiday	Time of Year or Date	Reason

Reading

Festival of the Full Moon

The following selection describes a festival in Thailand.

1. **Skim** *"Festival of the Full Moon" to get the main idea of each paragraph. Then write the paragraph numbers in the blanks next to the ideas.*

   a. _____ typical activities

   b. _____ history of the celebration

   c. _____ meaning of the celebration

Festival of the Full Moon

[1] *Loy Krathong* is my favorite holiday in Thailand because it is very beautiful and romantic. This is the celebration of the full moon in November. *Loy* means "float" and *Krathong* means "small, lotus-shaped boat." This is the day when we float *krathongs,* wash our sins away, and make wishes for the future.

[2] *Loy Krathong* began over 1,500 years ago. There was once a very kind and generous queen, Nopamas. She wanted to do something special for the king. Therefore, she made the first *krathong* out of banana stems and leaves and placed a lit candle, incense, and flowers in it. She gave the lotus-shaped boat to the king to float in the river. This was a way to thank the water spirits for the water and apologize for the pollution.

[3] Today, Thais clean the rivers to prepare for this day. Some people do good deeds—for example, giving money to the poor. There are contests, such as "Miss Nopamas" beauty contests and *krathong*-making contests. The most important part of the celebration is making *krathongs* and floating them lit with candles in the moonlight. Also, lovers believe that if they float *krathongs* together and the boats stay together in the water, their love will last forever.

2. *In exercise 1, you **skimmed** the reading to find the main ideas. Now read "Festival of the Full Moon" closely. Then complete the sentences. Write the numbers of the best endings in the blanks.*

    a. A *krathong* is a _____ .

        1. small floating lotus

        2. small floating boat shaped like a lotus

        3. floating boat made from a lotus

        4. boat made from a candle

b. Queen Nopamas wanted to _____.

1. float a *krathong* in the moonlight
2. wash her sins away
3. be the most beautiful woman
4. do something special for her husband

c. Typical *Loy Krathong* activities include all of the following except _____.

1. giving a gift to the king
2. making *krathongs*
3. beauty contests
4. giving money to poor people

3. *Match these words with their meanings.*

ANSWER KEY

a.	_____ sins	**1.**	garbage in the water or air
b.	_____ incense	**2.**	rest on the water
c.	_____ pollution	**3.**	bad things we do
d.	_____ float	**4.**	a substance that is sweet-smelling when burned

....

People around the world celebrate many holidays and traditions. What holidays do you usually celebrate?

Targeting

Ways to Describe Celebrations

1. *Read these sentences. Complete the second sentence in each item to describe holidays **you** celebrate.*

a. In **November** in **Thailand,** we have a celebration called **Loy Krathong.**

In _____the fall_____ in _____Korea_____ we have a
      (month/season)   (country/region)

celebration called _____Chusok_____.
           (name of celebration)

b. For me, the most important holiday is **New Year's.**

For me, the most important holiday is _____.
(name of holiday)

c. I like **Purim** because **it's a very happy holiday.**

I like _____ because _____.
(name of celebration)   (reason)

d. Coming of Age Day is important to us because **at 20 we become adults.**

_____ is important to us because
(name of celebration)

_____.
(reason)

e. We prepare **a special feast.**

We prepare _____.
(name of special food)

f. On this day **girls** give **chocolate bars** to **boys.**

On this day _____ give _____ to
(some people)   (something)

_____.
(someone)

Writing

Preparing to Write: Brainstorming a List

Before you write a description of a celebration, *brainstorm* a list of your ideas to help you get started.

What celebration do you want to write about?

1. *The list on the next page gives you some parts of a celebration description. Write your specific ideas next to each item to start your notes for the description.*

name of celebration	
meaning of name	
history	
date	
preparation for celebration	
traditional food	
traditional dances, music, songs	
traditional clothes	
gift giving	
typical activities	

2. *Decide on the order of ideas in your description. Number the items in the first column in exercise 1 to show the order.*
3. *What details do you think readers of your celebration description want to know? Add interesting details in the margins of the chart in exercise 1.*

Writing a Description of a Celebration

Now it's time to write about a celebration that you know.

Write a description of a celebration. Use your notes from Preparing to Write on pages 158–159.

Editing and Rewriting

Editing for Article and Noun Errors in Generalizations

When you make a generalization, you should always check the articles and nouns.

1. *Study these rules about articles and nouns.*

Rules	Examples
There are two common ways to make generalizations with count nouns. Use the indefinite article (*a, an*) with the singular noun, or make the noun plural. These two sentences have the same meaning.	**A** calendar represents the past. **Calendars** represent the past.
Do not use an article with noncount nouns.	Many customs are about good **luck**.

2. *Many of these sentences have errors in generalizations. Add an article or make a noun plural to correct these mistakes. Some sentences may be correct.*

(a) The New Year holiday is the most common celebration around the world. (b) Every culture has interesting New Year's tradition. (c) In many countries, custom focus on good luck for the new year and saying good-bye to the past. (d) In Peru and many other South American country, people put on yellow underwear. (e) No one knows where the custom comes from. (f) However, yellow has been the color of good luck for many generation. (g) Second Peruvian tradition is to eat twelve grape at midnight. (h) The grapes represent the twelve month of the year. (i) Some people say you must eat grape under table or without chewing them. (j) If you want to take trip in the new year, you must run around the block with packed suitcase. (k) Another interesting custom is to throw away old calendar. (l) In fact, if you are in Lima on December 31, at noon you will see calendar flying out of the windows!

> **EDITING TIP**
>
> Have someone else read your paper and mark where he or she would like more details.

Editing Checklist
Check the Content

1. *Exchange your celebration description with a classmate's. After you read your classmate's description, answer these questions.*

- ❑ Are there enough details?
- ❑ Can a reader picture the celebration?
- ❑ Are there transition words to show the order of events?

Check the Details

2. *Now, reread your description. If necessary, revise what you wrote. Then continue checking your own writing. Use these questions.*

   ❏ Did you use the past tense for events that happened in the past?
   ❏ Did you use the present tense to describe habits?
   ❏ Did you use the correct articles and noun forms in generalizations?

3. *Make your corrections and rewrite your description.*

Vocabulary Log

What words or phrases would you like to remember from this chapter? Write five to ten items in your notebook. Examples are on page 11.

Grammar and Punctuation Review

Look over your writing from this chapter. What changes did you need to make in grammar and punctuation? Write them in your notebook. Review them before the next writing assignment.

Class Activity   Hands-On Multicultural Celebration Experience

1 Give your classmates a hands-on experience from a different culture. Teach them how to make food for a traditional celebration, or to play a game, perform a dance, or sing a song from another culture.

or

2 Bring in traditional clothing or items for them to see.

or

3 Do a Web search for festivals and celebrations. Report your findings to the class.

Chapter 14

Take Your Daughter to Work Day

Special-interest days are organized by a lot of different groups in the United States. In this chapter, after you read about a special-interest day, you will write a summary.

Starting Point

··

On special-interest days (or weeks or months), different organizations encourage awareness of their causes or interests. They want the public to celebrate and learn about the topic of these days.

Highlighting Special Interests

ANSWER KEY

1. *Work with a partner. Which activities do you think would go best with these special-interest celebrations? Match the celebrations and the activities. Write the letters on the lines.*

Events		*Activity*
__d__	Multicultural Communication Month	**a.** picking up garbage along the highways
_____	Keep America Beautiful Month	**b.** returning overdue books to the library
_____	Secretaries' Week	**c.** listening to guitar music on the radio
_____	Library Forgiveness Week	**d.** learning about a celebration in another culture
_____	International Guitar Month	**e.** taking your secretary out to lunch

2. *If you were going to have a special-interest day, what would the topic be? Discuss with a partner.*

Reading

··

This selection describes a special-interest day in the workplace.

1. *Read about a special day for girls to learn about the world of work.*

Take Your Daughter to Work Day

Take Your Daughter to Work Day

[1] In the United States, we have Chocolate Week, Pay Your Bills Week, and Clean off Your Desk Day. Some special-interest days and weeks are humorous. Others are more serious, such as Black History Month, Stop the Violence and Save Our Kids Month, Keep America Beautiful Month, Be Kind to Animals Week, and Take Your Daughter to Work Day. About six million girls every year participate in this last event, but it has caused some disagreement in recent years.

[2] Boys learn early in life that they will work as adults. Many girls, on the other hand, often do not feel that they can succeed in the workplace. This is why Take Your Daughter to Work Day began in the early 1990s. On this day in April, 9- to 14-year-old girls watch women successfully working outside the home. The girls do not go to school. Instead, they go with their mothers, fathers, or other adults to their workplaces. A doctor may take his daughter to the hospital, or a female road worker may take her daughter to her job site.

[3] Not everyone is happy with Take Your Daughter to Work Day. Some bosses don't like having children at work. Some people think this day is not fair to boys. For this reason, some companies have changed the name of the day to *Take Your Child to Work Day.* Each year people suggest other ideas for a boys' day. One idea is Keep Our Sons at Home Day. On this day boys could learn about the work of homemaking and rearing children. These could be job possibilities for men as well as for women.

2. Writers often use pronouns or demonstrative adjectives to **refer** to nouns mentioned before. What do the underlined words in each item refer to? Scan the reading for these words and write their references on the lines.

ANSWER KEY

Paragraph		Item	Reference
a.	1	"this last celebration"	Take Your Daughter to Work Day
b.	1	"but it has"	_____
c.	2	"that they can succeed"	_____
d.	2	"On this day in April"	_____
e.	2	"their workplaces"	_____
f.	2	"her job site"	_____
g.	3	"this day is not fair"	_____
h.	3	"For this reason"	_____
i.	3	"On this day"	_____

3. According to "Take Your Daughter to Work Day," which of the following statements are true? Put a **T** for true and an **F** for false in the blanks.

ANSWER KEY

a. __T__ Some people think Take Your Daughter to Work Day is not right.

b. _____ Children have to go to school on Take Your Daughter to Work Day.

c. _____ The reason for Take Your Daughter to Work Day is to show girls possibilities for work outside the home.

d. _____ According to the author, homemaking and rearing children are jobs for boys, too.

Reflect on Reading

In exercise 2 you looked for words that pronouns and demonstrative adjectives **refer** to. Many words refer to other words in a reading. For example:

"They saw a sign on the highway. It said New York was sixty miles away."

In the second sentence, *it* refers to a word in the previous sentence. Is *it* the highway or the sign? You understand that *it* refers to the sign. Understanding **references** is an important reading skill. Below are common reference words.

Words	*Examples*
he, she, it, they	The car won't start. **It**'s stopped in the middle of the road. The Culbertsons couldn't be here tonight. **They** had another party to go to.
this, that, these, those	I stayed at a new hotel on the beach. **That** was the best part of my trip (**That** *refers to the activity of staying at the hotel on the beach.*) The large boxes need to be opened. **Those** over there contain the new computers.
one, another, the other, the first, the last, the former, the latter	There were two letters in the box. **The first/One** was from her parents. **The other** was an invitation to a party. There are different ways to deal with the problem. **One** way is to talk directly to the difficult person. **Another** is to talk to that person's manager. She made trips to Philadelphia and to New York last week. The **former** was for business and the **latter** was for pleasure.

A **summary** is a short version of the original writing. The steps in this section will help you write a summary, your next writing task.

1. *Look at these main ideas from "Take Your Daughter to Work Day." Underline the most important words. The first one has been done for you.*

    a. In the <u>United States</u>, we have <u>named a lot of special-interest dates</u>: Chocolate Week, Black History Month, Be Kind to Animals Week, Clean off Your Desk Day.

    b. About six million girls every year participate in one of these special-interest events, Take Your Daughter to Work Day.

    c. On this day in April, 9- to 14-year-old girls watch women successfully working outside the home.

    d. Take Your Daughter to Work Day began in the early 1990s because some people thought it was important to help girls feel that they can succeed in the workplace.

    e. Not everyone is happy with Take Your Daughter to Work Day because some people don't like having children at work and others think the day is not fair to boys.

    f. For this reason, some companies have changed the name of the day to *Take Your Child to Work Day,* and other people have suggested a Keep Our Sons at Home Day, when boys could learn about the work of homemaking and rearing children.

> **WRITING TIP**
>
> The first step in writing a summary is to find the most important elements.

2. *Look at the important elements you underlined in exercise 1. Which is the best sentence in each item below to say the idea **in different words**? Put a check (✓) on the line.*

    a:

    1. _____ Clean off Your Desk Day and Black History Month are examples of special-interest events.

    2. _____ There are a lot of "special-interest" days, weeks, or months in the United States.

    3. _____ We create a lot of dates.

> **WRITING TIP**
>
> When you write a summary, you need to use *your* words, not the author's.

b:

1. _____ One very popular special-interest event in the spring is Take Your Daughter to Work Day.

2. _____ About six million girls participate in Take Your Daughter to Work Day, one of these special-interest events.

3. _____ Take Your Daughter to Work Day is a special-interest day.

c:

1. _____ Girls 9 to 14 years old go to workplaces in the spring.

2. _____ Young and teenage girls see women in their workplaces on this day in the spring.

3. _____ Girls between the ages of 9 and 14 are able to see women working.

d:

1. _____ The people who started Take Your Daughter to Work Day thought that girls needed to see that they could succeed in jobs outside the home.

2. _____ Take Your Daughter to Work Day started in the early 1990s because some people thought it was an important idea.

3. _____ The organizers started Take Your Daughter to Work Day in the early 1990s because they wanted girls to see examples of women succeeding in the workplace.

e:

1. _____ Some people are unhappy about this day.

2. _____ Take Your Daughter to Work Day does not please some people.

3. _____ Some people don't like having children at work.

f:

1. _____ Some people want a Keep Our Sons at Home Day.

2. _____ Some people have decided to make changes in the activities of this day so that the focus is not only on girls.

3. _____ Some companies have included boys by changing the name to *Take Your Child to Work Day*.

Now you are ready to write a *summary*, a short version of a reading in different words.

Use your answers in Preparing to Write, exercise 2 (pages 167–168), to write a summary of the main ideas in "Take Your Daughter to Work Day." Add transition words to connect the ideas.

Vocabulary Log

What words or phrases would you like to remember from this chapter? Write five to ten items in your notebook. Examples are on page 11.

Grammar and Punctuation Review

Look over your writing from this chapter. What changes did you need to make in grammar and punctuation? Write them in your notebook. Review them before the next writing assignment.

Chapter 15

Special Events

It is customary for the organizers of events to send thank-you letters to people who help. In this chapter you will read about special events and write a formal letter to thank the community for their help with a special day.

Starting Point

·······································

Festival Themes

Festivals are often organized by a community or a local organization. They bring together people who enjoy a particular activity, such as dancing or watching movies.

What are these festivals for? Discuss with a partner or a small group.

New festivals and traditions in a community often focus on food and music.

1. **Scan** the following festival announcements to answer these questions. Try to do it in one minute.

ANSWER KEY

a. What area of the United States are these announcements

from? _____

b. Which festival runs the longest number of days?

_____

c. Where can you see chefs demonstrate cooking techniques?

_____

d. Who is the organizer of two of these festivals?

_____

e. How much is admission to the Garlic Festival?

_____

f. Which festival is organized by a religious institution?

_____

g. Which festival can probably handle the most cars?

_____

> ### READING TIP
>
> When you read, you don't always need to read every word. When you **scan** something, you just look for specific information.

April 15; Sunday
11:00 a.m. to 6:00 p.m.

Taste of Kosher L.A.
Sample the best of kosher cuisine in the beautiful University of Judaism at the top of Mulholland Drive. Kosher wines, jazz and folk bands, and fun for the kids. Free admission.

University of Judaism
15600 Mulholland Drive
Los Angeles, CA
818/771-8777

June 21–23; Fri.
5:00 p.m.–12:00 a.m.;
Sat. 12:00 p.m.–12:00 a.m.;
Sun. 12:00 p.m. – 10:00 p.m.

Taste of Orange County
Southern California's largest food and music festival featuring forty of Orange County's finest restaurants and sixty musical acts on four outdoor stages. Admission: $8 (adults); $3 (children 3–12); under 3, free. Unlimited on-site free parking.

Irvine Marine Corps Air Station El Toro
El Toro, CA
JW Events: Dennis Yeomans
714/753-1551

July 6–7 & 13–14;
Sat. 12:00 p.m.–10:00 p.m.;
Sun. 12:00 p.m. – 10:00 p.m.

Garlic Festival
13th Annual Los Angeles Garlic Festival on the Federal Building Lawn in Westwood. An array of the best restaurants and chefs offering a variety of culinary delights. Entertainment, laser shows, lottery, chef demos, and more. Free.

West Los Angeles
Federal Building
Wilshire Blvd. & Veteran Avenue, Los Angeles, CA
Garlic Festival Productions:
Kathy Veniero
310/274-2043

August 9, 10, & 11; Fri.
5:00 p.m.–12:00 a.m.;
Sat. 12:00 p.m.–12:00 a.m.;
Sun. 12:00 p.m. – 10:00 p.m.

L.A. a la Carte
L.A.'s premier food and music festival featuring thirty-five of the city's finest restaurants and more than forty musical acts on three outdoor stages. Admission is $8 for adults, $3 for children 3–12; children under 3, free.

UCLA's lot 32, corner of Wilshire Blvd. & Veteran Avenue, Westwood, CA
JW Events: Dennis Yeomans
714/753-1551
The Gas Company

You just *scanned* the festival announcements. In which of these situations would you probably scan?

| Looking up a word in a dictionary | Reading a mystery novel | Reading the directions for a new computer |

2. *Scan* this Web site. Look for the answers to the questions and write them on the lines.

a. Where is the festival? _____

b. How big is the festival? _____

c. When is it held? _____

Celebrate the Northwest's diverse heritage at the
NORTHWEST FOLKLIFE FESTIVAL!

General Information

In Seattle, Washington, one of the most popular celebrations is the Northwest Folklife Festival. This festival celebrates the Northwest's diverse heritage. With more than 6,000 participants from over 100 countries, 18 stages, 1,000 performances, and an audience of nearly 200,000, the Folklife Festival is one of the largest festivals in the region. The Folklife Festival is always held on Memorial Day weekend (the weekend that includes the last Monday in May). Founded in 1972, the Northwest Folklife Festival is one of the nation's largest free events and is truly a celebration for everyone.

INDEX TO THE GENERAL INFORMATION PAGE

- Festival Dates And Times
- *i* General Program Information
- Educational Programs
- Instrument Auction
- The Northwest Folklife Festival Souvenir Program
- ? How To Participate
- Practical Information
- Getting To The Festival
- At The Festival

3. *Now, read the Northwest Folklife Festival Web page more carefully. Answer these questions.*

    a. What kind of festival is it? _____

    b. How many people attend the festival? _____

    c. When was the first Folklife Festival held? _____

    d. How much does it cost to attend? _____

    e. Where would you look to find more information about

        1. the time the festival opens _____

        2. which bus to take to the festival _____

        3. the schedule of events _____

        4. how to apply to perform in the festival _____

Reading 2

Sponsors

Businesses and individuals in a community often give support to a cause, such as a special-interest day, week, or month. Support can be money, donations of facilities, advertising, and other methods of helping. These supporters are called *sponsors*.

1. *Read the following newspaper article on Keep Our Community Clean Week.*

Town Center in Full Bloom

Garfield. If you've driven through the center of town lately, you may have noticed a new look this spring. Residents have recently completed Keep Our Community Clean Week, and their efforts have really paid off. The week started with a kickoff breakfast to encourage everyone to begin a week of cleaning up and planting. Mayor Bingham joined in the events by agreeing to take a pie in the face for every 100 pounds of litter that was picked up. You can bet that that challenge really inspire everyone to pick up litter. Thanks to him and other sponsors in the community, the community looks clean and neat. There are dozens of new trees planted and the tulips are in full bloom. A big thanks to Jane Nash and her organizing committee. This accomplishment is yet another example of what we can do together to make our community more livable.

2. *Here are two lists: a list of the sponsors and a list of gifts. Which sponsors gave which support? With a classmate, match the person or business in the left column with the kind of support in the right column. Write the letters on the lines.*

____ Ferguson's Hardware Store (24 Maple Street)	**a.** tree seedlings and 500 tulip bulbs
____ tellers at First National Freestone Bank (11534 120th Avenue)	**b.** free photocopying of the flyer
_a_ Skyway Yard and Garden Supply (14 Old Silver Lake Road)	**c.** a challenge: He would take a pie in his face for every 100 pounds of litter picked up
____ Fast Copy Center (555 University Avenue)	**d.** large litter bags
____ Mayor Bingham (City Hall, 2008 4th Avenue)	**e.** a kickoff breakfast for the community

Writing

Preparing to Write 1: Analyzing Organization

To help you understand how information in a formal letter is organized, look at an example of a formal thank-you letter.

Read the following formal thank-you letter. Match the descriptions listed below with the parts of the letter. Write a part on each line.

date
the sender's name and address
greeting
the sponsor's name and address
a closing

signature
a brief report of the success
   of the week
the thank-you message
the writer's name

A formal letter has certain formats. The example here shows one format. For more information about how to write a formal letter, see pages 210–211 in Reference.

_____ *Date*

_____

_____

_____

_____

_____

_____

November 5, 1997

Jane Nash
20043 N.E. 156th Avenue
Garfield, OH 45710

Mayor Bingham
City Hall
2008 4th Avenue
Garfield, OH 45710

Dear Mayor Bingham:

I'm writing on behalf of the organizers of Keep Our Community Clean Week. We really appreciated your support for this cleanup project. We are sorry that you are got so many pies in your face, but your challenge attracted many people to our event.

During Keep Our Community Clean Week, we picked up 900 pounds of litter. Now we enjoy a clean and beautiful town center, and residents have begun to recognize that the problem of garbage is serious.

Thank you very much for your help.

Sincerely,

Jane Nash

Jane Nash
Chairperson, Keep Our Community Clean Week.

Preparing to Write 2: Formal Thank-You Expressions

Your next assignment is to write a formal thank-you letter to a sponsor of Keep Our Community Clean Week. Certain thank-you expressions are typical of formal letters.

1. *Here are some typical thank-you expressions. Complete these sentences about the sponsors and their support from the list on page 174.*

   a. *(to Skyway Yard and Garden Supply)* Thank you for

      the tree seedlings and tulip bulbs .

   b. *(to Ferguson's Hardware Store)* We really appreciated your

      gift of _____ .

   c. *(to the mayor of the town)* We are sorry that you

      _____ ,

      but we really appreciated your _____ .

   d. *(to the tellers at First National Freestone Bank)* Thank you

      very much for _____ .

   e. *(to Fast Copy Center)* We'd really like to thank you for

      _____ .

Writing a Formal Thank-You Letter

1. *Choose a sponsor for Keep Our Community Clean Week from those listed on page 174. Review the formal letter format on page 175. Write a formal thank-you letter.*

   or

2. *On a separate paper, write a formal thank-you letter to an organization or individual who has done something helpful for you or for someone you know.*

....

Here are two things to remember about formal letters.

1. The language in formal letters should be polite and more formal than everyday conversation.
2. In a formal thank-you letter, the focus should be on the reader, not on the sender.

Work with a partner. Which sentence or group of sentences in each pair is appropriate for a formal thank-you letter, and why? Circle the number and discuss your choices.

a. **1.** I had a good time. It was a great week. Thanks a lot!
    2. Everyone helped out, and Keep Our Community Clean Week was very successful. Thank you very much for your support.

b. **1.** We had a good time and enjoyed Keep Our Community Clean Week. Your support made a big difference. We look forward to your support next year.
    2. We had a good time and enjoyed Keep Our Community Clean Week. Your support made a big difference. Help us next year.

c. **1.** Come visit our town center in the spring. The trees and tulips will be beautiful then.
    2. Please come visit our town center in the spring. The trees and tulips will be beautiful then.

d. **1.** At first, people didn't want to pick up litter, but they imagined seeing you with a pie in your face and worked very hard. Everyone really appreciated your interesting challenge.
    2. At first, people didn't want to pick up litter, but they imagined you with a pie in your face and worked very hard.

Editing for Appropriate Language in Formal Letters

ANSWER KEY

Editing Checklist

Check the Content

1. *Exchange your formal thank-you letter with a classmate's. After you read your classmate's letter, answer these questions.*

   - ❏ Is it clear what event or contribution the thank-you is for?
   - ❏ Is there a thank-you paragraph and a summary of the event's success?
   - ❏ Is the language polite?
   - ❏ Is the letter formal?
   - ❏ Does the thank-you focus on the reader?

Check the Details

2. *Now, reread your letter. If necessary, revise what you wrote. Try to change any informal words or expressions to more formal ones. Add more information if necessary. Then continue checking your own letter. Use these questions.*

   - ❏ Did you include a greeting and a closing?
   - ❏ Did you write your signature?

3. *Make your corrections and rewrite your thank-you letter.*

Vocabulary Log

What words or phrases would you like to remember from this chapter? Write five to ten items in your notebook. Examples are on page 11.

Grammar and Punctuation Review

Look over your writing from this chapter. What changes did you need to make in grammar and punctuation? Write them in your notebook. Review them before the next writing assignment.

6 Getting Down to Work

Most people work for a living. Some people like their jobs, and others would rather do different work. Work can be rewarding, but it can also be a cause of stress. Whatever the situation, work is important in most people's lives.

Here are some of the activities you will do in this unit:

- Read about volunteer work in the United States
- Write a business letter to describe a volunteer project
- Read people's preferences about working versus not working
- Take a survey and report on the results
- Read about one businessperson's decision
- Read newspaper advertisements for jobs

Chapter 16

Work for No Pay?

Many people do volunteer work. In this chapter you will read about volunteerism and design a program for volunteers. You will also write a letter asking for volunteers.

Starting Point

Volunteering

Volunteer means to "give help without getting paid."

1. *Look at the photographs below and answer the questions with a partner or small group.*

   a. What are the people doing?
   b. Who benefits from this volunteer work?

2. *How about you? Do you have any experience as a volunteer? Discuss this with a classmate.*

....

This selection gives information about volunteering in the United States.

1. *Read the following selection.*

Volunteerism in America

[1] Thomas Jones is a lawyer in Miami. Every Saturday he spends the day with a 10-year-old named Luther Jefferson. Thomas is not related to Luther, but he is his Big Brother. Big Brothers (and Big Sisters) spend time with children from single-parent families. Wanda Zaleski is a high school student in Chicago. Two afternoons a week, Wanda goes to a home for old people. She reads books and plays the piano for the people in the home. Thomas and Wanda are both volunteers. They like to work with people.

[2] Unusual? No. Even Jimmy Carter, former president of the United States, volunteers. He puts on his work clothes, picks up a hammer, and works with a volunteer group to build housing for low-income people. About 50 percent of adults in the United States volunteer three to five hours a week. Young people volunteer as well. In a poll of 1,400 12- to 17-year-olds, 61 percent of them volunteered an average of 3.2 hours a week.

[3] Volunteer work has unlimited possibilities. Many people work with children or young people. They volunteer in their children's schools. They coach their children's sports teams or run after-school programs for teenagers. Like Jimmy Carter, many people also help those in need. You don't have to work with people to volunteer. Some people clean up an area of highway or build a trail. They even help scientists by tagging wildlife or digging for dinosaur bones.

[4] Why do people volunteer? Volunteer work makes people feel happy. They are making a difference. They can use their talents and abilities in different ways. They also enjoy being part of the community by meeting new people in their cities or neighborhoods.

[5] Some companies encourage volunteering. Forty-five percent of the employees at IBM, a huge computer company, volunteer. Many managers think highly of people who volunteer. Managers believe these employees have more balanced lives when they are volunteers outside of work. Some companies even give employees time off to do volunteer work!

2. *What is the topic in each paragraph?* **Scan** *the reading and write the paragraph numbers on the lines next to the correct headings.*

    a. _____ why people volunteer   **d.** __1__ life as a volunteer

    b. _____ statistics about   **e.** _____ possibilities for
                   volunteerism   volunteering

    c. _____ company support

3. *Read these sentences about information in the reading. Put a* **T** *in the blank if the sentence is true and an* **F** *if it is false.*

    a. _____ There are limited opportunities for volunteering.

    b. _____ Some businesses think positively about employees who volunteer.

    c. _____ Sixty-one percent of all 12- to 17-year-olds in the United States volunteer.

    d. _____ Jimmy Carter was once president of the United States.

    e. _____ Wanda Zaleski gets paid for her work in the home for old people.

    f. _____ About half the adults in the United States volunteer eight hours each week.

    g. _____ People can choose from many different volunteer options.

4. *Work with a partner. Which of the following is the best summary of the article? Discuss your choice.*

    a. Companies encourage workers to volunteer, and volunteers enjoy the opportunities to meet people and to help others.

    b. Thomas Jones, Wanda Zaleski, and even a former president of the United States volunteer. This shows how common volunteering is in the United States.

    c. Volunteerism is quite common in the United States, where 50 to 60 percent of the population volunteers in some way or another.

182 Unit 6 • *Getting Down to Work*

5. *Complete these sentences with the words from "Volunteerism in America." If you aren't sure about the meaning of a word, look for it in the reading and use context clues to help you.*

ability	housing	trails
coach	make a difference	unlimited
community	poll	volunteer

a. Everyone was excited about building a new ___*community*___ center.

b. A lot of poor people lived in the old hotel. When the owners decided to sell it, many people lost their _____.

c. In her volunteer job, Wanda can use her _____ to play the piano.

d. Sometimes I feel as if I'm wasting my time. I don't know if I _____ when I volunteer.

e. They _____ three hours a week at the school.

f. In the city, tourists often follow walking _____ to see interesting or famous sites.

g. The _____ showed that few people are interested in volunteering, but I have a hard time believing that.

h. I would like to _____ the soccer team, but I don't have time.

i. We had to be careful how much we spent. We didn't have an _____ supply of money!

Writing

Preparing to Write: Determining the Focus

Volunteers can help with many different projects. Groups of people just like you start volunteer projects! After you figure out what the project involves, the most important step is writing the call for volunteers.

1. *Prepare notes for your writing. Answer these questions with a partner or in a small group.*

   a. What volunteer programs do you know of? _____

   _____

   b. What kinds of problems are there in your area? List any you can think of (for example, *dirty streets, low literacy*).

   _____   _____   _____

   c. Choose one problem that volunteers could help with.

   _____

   d. What would the volunteers actually do? _____

   _____

   e. Who would be the best volunteers? Young people? The

   elderly? Parents? Anyone? _____

   f. Do the volunteers need to have any special qualifications or

   skills? _____

Writing a Promotional Letter

WRITING TIP

Don't forget to write using formal letter format!

Write a letter to the local TV and radio stations in your area. Ask them to announce information about your call for volunteers. You need to describe your program. Use your notes from Preparing to Write. Include information about how volunteers can contact you (a telephone number or a meeting time and place).

For both reading and writing, it is important to know the difference between *adjectives* and *adverbs*.

Editing for Word Forms: Adjectives and Adverbs

1. *Study these rules and examples.*

Rules	Examples	
An **adjective** is a word that gives information about a noun.	We took a **slow** train. I had a **volunteer** job.	
An **adverb** gives information about a verb or about an adjective. Adverbs usually end in **-ly** or **-ily**.	I drove **slowly** because of the rain. I did it **voluntarily.** The movie was **terribly** sad.	
These are some irregular adverb forms.	*Adjective* good fast hard	*Adverb* well fast hard

2. *Complete these sentences with the adjective or adverb in parentheses.*

a. The child ran _____quickly_____ across the room.   (quick, quickly)

ANSWER KEY

b. The grocery store provided _____ food to a community organization.   (free, freely)

c. Everyone wanted to help. They _____ gave money and time.   (eager, eagerly)

d. When people heard about the emergency, they

_____ started sending money and supplies. (immediate, immediately)

e. They sent it before anyone even asked for it. They sent it

_____. (voluntary, voluntarily)

f. People are _____ when they do volunteer work. (happy, happily)

3. *Put a check (✓) in front of the sentence(s) that use(s) adjectives or adverbs correctly.*

    a. _____ They worked **good** together.

    b. _____ They collected food from grocery stores and gave it to **needy** families.

    c. _____ Please tell me your **honestly** opinion.

    d. _____ It was **incredibly hard** work.

    e. _____ The **sad** truth is that no one is going to volunteer to help.

    f. _____ Everyone contributed **willing** to the project.

Editing Checklist

Check the Content

1. *Exchange your promotional letter with a classmate. After you read your class-mate's letter, answer these questions.*

Do you understand:
- ❏ Why this is an important volunteer project?
- ❏ What the problem is?
- ❏ The qualifications (if any) that are necessary?
- ❏ How people can contact the organizers?

Check the Details

2. *Now, reread your letter. If necessary, revise what you wrote. Add more information and try to change unclear words or sentences. Then continue checking your own writing. Use these questions.*

- ❏ Did you include information about how people can contact you?
- ❏ Did you include information about who should volunteer?
- ❏ Does your letter follow an appropriate formal letter format?
- ❏ Check the adjectives and adverbs. Did you use the correct forms?

3. *Make your corrections and rewrite your letter.*

Vocabulary Log

What words or phrases would you like to remember from this chapter? Write five to ten items in your notebook. Examples are on page 11.

Grammar and Punctuation Review

Look over your writing from this chapter. What changes did you need to make in grammar and punctuation? Write them in your notebook. Review them before the next writing assignment.

Chapter 17

Would
I Work?

Some people work when they don't have to. Would you? In this chapter, you will read job announcements and a report on people's preferences to work. You will also write your own report.

Starting Point

A Selection of Jobs

1. *Work with a classmate. Match the jobs in the pictures with the job titles in the list.*

classroom teacher   machinist
construction worker   medical technician
data processor   police officer
graphic design artist   potter

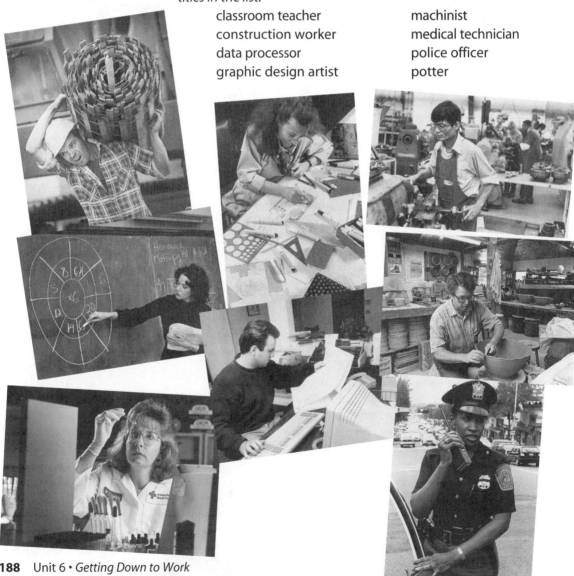

2. *What do you think about these jobs? Discuss the following questions with a partner or a small group.*

    a. Which job do you think has the highest status?

    b. Which job requires the most training?

    c. Which job gives people the greatest satisfaction?

    d. Which job(s) will probably not be around in the second half of the twenty-first century?

Reading 1

....

Have you ever looked for a job in the newspaper? This selection is from the employment section of a newspaper.

Help Wanted Ads

1. *Scan the following "Help Wanted" advertisements.*

CONSTRUCTION Laborer
Full time. Must have tools and a vehicle. $8/hr (206) 555-5555.

Cruise Ship Restaurant Workers—Opportunities to travel! Pacific Cruise Lines restaurant hiring:
• Assistant Manager
• Kitchen Manager
• Wait Staff
• Dish/Busser
• Line Cooks
Apply at dock, 120 Harbor Drive, 7 a.m.–3 p.m.

EXECUTIVE SECRETARY —for medical management firm. Must have excellent computer skills. Availability to work late and/or weekends occasionally. Must have professional manner and appearance, strong telephone and people skills. Must be flexible, a team player, prompt and reli-able. Exc. benefits. Please send resume and cover letter to P.O. Box 26730, Kirkland, WA 98033

MAILING MACHINE OPERATORS
Large mailing company seeks machine operators to fill positions in Letter-shop. Exp. with Bell & Howell, Cheshire, and/or Baum folder equipment preferred, but will train right candidate. Salary DOE. Submit cover letter and resume to: Human Resources, Kent Mailing, 6600 S. 231st St., Kent, WA 98032.

Research
RESEARCH TECHNICIAN
Skilled technician needed to conduct laboratory research experiments. Requirements include Bachelor's degree in bio-logical science; min 1–2 yrs lab experience involv-ing molecular biology; demonstrated effective written, verbal, & inter-personal communication skills; & ability to work weekends or holidays as required. FT position. Qualified candidates may send resume by fax to (804) 555-5555.

Robotics
ENGINEERS ROBOTICS ENGINEERS
needed by large manufac-turing company. Experi-ence with redesigning manufacturing produc-tion lines important. Fax resume to 805-999-5555.

Sales—New Day Media is currently accepting ap-plications for the position of Entry Level Account Executive. A 4-year degree in an applicable business-related field is pref'd. Send resume to: New Day Media, 190 7th Ave., Suite 400, Seattle, WA 98109. No phone calls please.

ANSWER KEY

2. *Answer the questions about the reading.*

    a. *Find a job that involves the following activities. Write the head-line or job title(s) from the ad.*

        office work   _____

        work in a lab   _____

        travel   _____

        skilled labor   _____

        sales   _____

        work with
        tools or   _____
        machines

    b. *Which job(s) require(s) the most education?*

         _____

    c. *Liam Chong is looking for a job. He just finished a two-year degree in business, and he has a lot of computer experience. Which job is the best match for his background?*

         _____

    d. *Do you think any of these jobs will **not** be around in fifty years? Write them here.*

         _____

         _____

....

This newspaper article reports on what choices people would make if they didn't have to work.

Who Would Work?

1. *Read the following selection.*

— WHO WOULD WORK? —

In a recent survey, people were asked about how much they would work if they had all the money they needed. The answers were surprising. Twenty-one percent of men said that they would like to do full-time family care. The percentage of women who would stay at home full-time if they could afford it dropped from 39 percent in 1981 to 31 percent in this survey.

When asked about other options, 33 percent of men and 15 percent of women said they would work full-time. Twenty-eight percent of men and 33 percent of women preferred the idea of part-time work. Volunteer work appealed to 20 percent of women and 17 percent of men.

Family life is more complicated for families with two breadwinners. Many women work both outside the home and as homemakers. However, 56 percent of the women polled did not want to give up either role. They liked having responsibilities both at home and at work.

2. *Using context clues, find words in the article with the same meaning as these words. Write them on the lines.*

a. people who make money to support a family _____

_____

b. work for no pay

_____

c. not long ago

_____

d. be able to do (something) financially _____

_____

e. possibilities

_____

f. hard to figure out

_____

g. duties and obligations

_____

3. _Which statement in each pair is true about these sentences using information from "Who Would Work?" Circle the number._

a. Family life is more complicated for families with two bread-winners.

  1. Family life is more difficult when both spouses bring home money.
  2. Family life is more difficult when both spouses have to work.

b. People were asked how much they would work.

  1. The researchers wanted to study how many hours people work.
  2. The researchers asked people about a possibility or an ideal situation.

c. Twenty-one percent of men said that they would like to do full-time family care.

  1. Twenty-one percent stay home to take care of their families.
  2. Twenty-one percent do not stay home, but they are interested in the idea.

d. The percentage of women who would stay at home full-time if they could afford it dropped from 39 percent in 1981 to 31 percent in this survey.

  1. Thirty-one percent of women wish that they could stay home.
  2. In this survey, more women want to stay home full-time now than in 1981.

e. Thirty-three percent of men and 15 percent of women said that they would work full-time.

  1. More men than women like the idea of full-time work.
  2. Thirty-three percent of men work full-time.

4. ***Taking notes in a diagram or chart*** *is a helpful reading skill.*
Complete the chart with statistics from the reading.

ANSWER KEY

If They Had Enough Money to Live as Comfortably as They Would Like, What Would They Do?	Women	Men
full-time family care	_____ %	_____ %
full-time work	_____ %	_____ %
part-time work	_____ %	_____ %
volunteer work	_____ %	_____ %

READING TIP

When you reread something to find specific information, think about what the information should look like. This will help you find the information more quickly.

· ·

Targeting

When you gather information—for example, in a survey—you need to report your results.

Expressions for Reporting Results

ANSWER KEY

1. *Look again at paragraph 1 of "Who Would Work?" Complete the expressions or sentences to report the results.*

a. _____*in*_____ a recent ____*survey*____

b. people _____ _____ about

c. _____ _____ men said

d. The percentage _____ _____ dropped

_____ 39 percent _____ 31 percent _____

this _____ .

ANSWER KEY

2. *Make the best choice to complete these sentences. Write the numbers on the lines.*

a. _____ They would work even if they

b. _____ I would like to have a part-time

c. _____ Building houses is

d. _____ Fifty percent of

e. _____ Twenty-five

f. _____ I volunteer

g. _____ We go to work every day to

h. _____ They said that they

i. _____ We conducted

j. _____ We would like to do

1. the people we surveyed said yes to item 6.

2. of the people said no.

3. earn enough money to live on.

4. had enough money to live on.

5. volunteer work.

6. hard work.

7. at the Center for the Blind.

8. job.

9. a survey.

10. wanted to work.

Writing

Preparing to Write: Survey

Most people have to work, but it's interesting to think about what you would do if you didn't have to!

1. *Discuss this question with a classmate. Then put a check (✓) next to the statement that applies.*

Imagine you do not need to work. You have enough money to live a comfortable life. Would you work anyway?

❑ Yes, I would work full-time.

❑ No, I would do full-time family care.

❑ I would work part-time.

❑ I would do volunteer work.

❑ _____
     (other)

2. *Poll your classmates. Figure out the percentages and write them in this chart.*

	Women	*Men*	*Total*
full-time work			
full-time family care			
part-time work			
volunteer work			
other			

3. *Complete these sentences to introduce your survey results. Use the information from the poll in exercise 2.*

a. The _____ class conducted a poll to find out

what people would do if they _____

_____.

b. The results of the poll were _____

_____.

4. *Now complete these sentences to report on your survey results.*

a. Most of the people surveyed (_____ percent) said that they

_____.

b. Another _____ percent said that they _____

_____.

c. Only _____ percent preferred to _____.

Writing a Report

Write the results of your poll in a newspaper report. You will need to add more details to the information you completed in Preparing to Write, exercises 2, 3, and 4, if there were significant differences between men's and women's responses.

Editing and Rewriting

Editing Verb Tenses in a Report

Always check the verb tenses in your writing. Be especially careful when you report what other people have said.

1. *Study these rules.*

Rules	Examples
The past tense is commonly used to write a report.	We **took** a poll in our class.
The past tense usually follows a past reporting verb (*said, reported,* and so on).	They said (that) they **wanted** to work.
Carry on with the same tense, even if you don't use a reporting verb in each sentence.	No one **preferred** to stay home with the children.
Use *would prefer* or *would like* to report on someone's preference.	Ten men said they **would like** to stay home. They **would prefer** to stay home.
Sometimes you will have a mix of tenses.	She **said** that she **would like** to work in education because she **wants** (or **wanted**) to work with children.

2. *Put a check (✓) in front of the sentence(s) with correct verb forms.*

ANSWER KEY

a. _____ They said that they would like to stay home.

b. _____ We survey twenty people.

c. _____ We asked if they would prefer to stay home.

d. _____ Ten percent of the people we surveyed are women.

e. _____ Ninety percent were men.

3. *Correct the errors in the verbs in these sentences. There may not be a mistake in every sentence.*

ANSWER KEY

(a) The writing class conducted a poll to find out what people do if they didn't have to work. (b) The results of the poll were surprising. (c) No one wants to stay home full-time. (d) No women want to be responsible only for their families. (e) Eighty percent of the men prefer to work part-time. (f) Only 12 percent of the women choose this option.

(g) The writing class conducted a survey to find out what people will do if they had enough money to live a comfortable life. (h) Only 16 percent prefer to do volunteer work. (i) More women than men would choose to work, even if they didn't have to.

(j) When asked about other options, another 31 percent said that they want to do full-time work. (k) We find that 15 percent of the people we polled wanted to spend all their time on leisure activities. (l) Forty percent of the people we poll were women.

Editing Checklist

Check the Content
1. *Exchange your report with a classmate. After you read your classmate's report, answer these questions.*

❑ How clear is the report?
❑ Is there an introduction and a conclusion to the information in the report?

Check the Details

2. *Now, reread your report. If necessary, revise what you wrote. Add an introduction and a conclusion. Add more details, if necessary. Then continue checking your own writing. Use these questions.*

    ☐ Check the verbs. Did you use the correct tense?
    ☐ Check any expressions from Targeting: Expressions to Report Results, exercise 2, on page 194. Are they correct?

3. *Make your corrections and rewrite your report.*

Vocabulary Log

What words or phrases would you like to remember from this chapter? Write five to ten items in your notebook. Examples are on page 11.

Grammar and Punctuation Review

Look over your writing from this chapter. What changes did you need to make in grammar and punctuation? Write them in your notebook. Review them before the next writing assignment.

Class Activity   Job Profiles

1 With a partner or a small group, think of people with interesting or unusual jobs. Try to think of people you see in your daily life.

2 Arrange to talk with one or two of these people.

3 What do you want to find out? Make a list of questions—for example, how did the person first get interested in the job? Or how does he or she like the job? Or what are the advantages and disadvantages of the job?

4 Report to the class about your discussion.

5 You may want to write about the people you interviewed and make a class book of all the articles.

Chapter 18

Hard Decisions

Starting Point

The life of a company employee is not always easy. Neither is the life of a company owner, as the reading in this chapter illustrates.

Property Loss

Look at the photo and discuss these questions with a partner or a small group.

1. What kind of building burned down?
2. What happens when a business burns down? Consider the owner, the employees, and the insurance company.

Reading

Malden Mills

In the report that follows, you will find out more about the fire in the photo.

1. Read "Malden Mills" and answer the questions that follow each paragraph. As you read each paragraph, cover the rest of the reading so that you won't look ahead.

Malden Mills

READING TIP

Good readers think ahead as they read. They try to **predict** what they will read next.

[1] In December of 1996, a boiler exploded at Malden Mills. Malden Mills made fleece fabric for sports clothes. Its customers were huge companies like L.L. Bean, Patagonia, and Lands End. The owner of the mill, Aaron Feuerstein, was 70 years old at the time of the fire. Many people gave Feuerstein advice, such as "Close the mill." "Sell it!" "Move it to a place where labor is cheaper." "Take the insurance money and move to the Bahamas."

2. **Predict.** *What do you think Mr. Feuerstein did? Write your ideas here.*

_____

_____

_____

_____

3. *Read on to see if your ideas were right.*

[2] However, Mr. Feuerstein did none of those things. Within days of the fire, Feuerstein gave his employees amazing news. Not only would he rebuild the plant, he would also pay 1,400 jobless workers their full salaries and benefits. This he did for three months while he worked to start production again in other buildings.

4. *Don't look ahead yet. Make another **prediction.** What do you think the last paragraph of the reading is about?*

_____

_____

_____

_____

5. *Read on to see if you were right.*

[3] Within a year, 85 percent of the workers at Malden Mills were back at work. Rebuilding cost Feuerstein 15 million dollars in wages and benefits. Feuerstein was a hero to many people. Other people thought he was a fool.

6. *What do you think? Was Feuerstein a fool? A hero? A smart business-person? Write your opinion here. Then discuss these questions and your opinions with a partner or a small group.*

---

7. *Now read comments that people made about Feuerstein. Which one is closest to your opinion? Discuss with a classmate.*

　　a. "I've never seen a man who cared more about his employees."

　　b. "At 70 years old, I think he should have taken the insurance money and sold the rest of the plant."

　　c. "He's not a fool. He had a business that brought in 20 million dollars a year in profits. His greatest asset was his skilled employees. Lose them and you lose the business. This company can continue to bring in 20 million dollars a year for years to come."

Reflect on Reading

In exercises 2 and 4 you made **predictions.** When you predict, you combine your background knowledge and experience with information about the current situation. This prepares you to understand what you read next and to guess what might come next.

8. _Understanding words in context_ _is an important reading skill. Read the sentences in the left column. Then make the best choice to complete the sentence or answer the question in the right column. Write the number of the answer on the line._

a. A boiler exploded at Malden Mills.

A *boiler* is probably _____.
1. a bomb
2. a piece of equipment
3. an area of the production line

b. Malden Mills made fleece fabric for sports clothes.

Fleece is a type of fabric.

True or false? _____

c. The cost of labor is cheaper.

Another word for *labor* is _____.
1. workers
2. production
3. energy

d. He paid workers their full salaries and benefits.

An example of a *benefit* is _____.
1. money
2. a job
3. health insurance

e. He paid workers their full salaries and benefits.

A synonym for *salaries* is _____.
1. wages
2. income
3. retirement money

9. _Which word in each line across doesn't fit with the others? Cross it out._

a. made	sold	produced
b. customers	buyers	owners
c. workers	wages	employees
d. production	salaries	benefits
e. factory	boiler	plant

Quickwriting: Good Qualities of a Company

Aaron Feuerstein's employees probably think that he is a wonderful employer. Think about situations that you know. What makes a company a good place to work? In your notebook, write for five to ten minutes about this topic.

Transition words help you make your writing clear. Here are some transitions that show contrast.

Transitions That Show Contrast

1. *Study the information about transitions.*

Rules	Examples
Transitions usually occur at the beginning of a sentence or independent clause, followed by a comma.	I like my coworkers. **However,** I don't like my job. **On the one hand,** I would like to stay, but, **on the other hand,** I don't think I can stand it any longer. It's a good job. **On the other hand,** I'm really tired of the long commute.
But and **so** are conjunctions. They join two sentences and have a comma before them.	I want to work in an office, **so** I am taking some computer courses. The job pays well, **but** the benefits don't include health insurance.
Compared to/with is followed by a noun or noun phrase.	**Compared to my last job,** this one is easy. **Compared with her last two books,** this one is long.

2. *Complete the sentences with expressions from this list. You may use them more than once.*

on the one hand   however   compared to (with)
on the other hand   but   so

a. Construction work is very hard labor. _____*However,*_____

it usually pays well.

b. Construction work is very hard labor, _____

it usually pays well.

c. I don't know whether I would want to work on a cruise ship.

_____, you would get to travel to interesting

places. _____, the jobs don't pay very well.

d. _____ other jobs in this list, work on a cruise

ship sounds the most interesting.

e. Working in an office sounds interesting to me.

_____, I cannot type or use a computer.

f. Most of the jobs in this list require training or experience.

_____, some of the cruise ship restaurant

jobs don't.

g. The sales job looks interesting, but some salespeople spend

all day just making telephone calls, _____ it

may not really be very interesting at all.

h. I have a degree in biological science, _____ I

don't have experience, _____ I won't apply

for the research technician job.

i. I am interested in the executive secretary job.

_____, I don't want to work on weekends.

3. *Reread the job ads on page 189. Write sentences about six of these jobs. Use the transition words in exercise 2.*

a. _____

_____

b. _____

_____

c. _____

_____

d. _____

_____

e. _____

_____

f. _____

_____

Writing

Preparing to Write: Supporting Your Opinion

In this unit, you have read a lot about jobs and the possibilities for working. In the next writing assignment, you need to give your opinion about the best job for yourself.

With a partner or a small group, answer and discuss the following questions.

1. If you could have any job in the world, what would that job be? _____

2. Why? What are the advantages of that job? List them here.

_____

_____

_____

_____

3. Why would you be good at that job?

_____

_____

_____

_____

Writing a Self-Evaluation

Write an explanation of why you would be well-qualified for the job you chose in Preparing to Write. This could be a self-evaluation or a "cover letter" (enclosing your resumé) that you would write in a job application process. If you want, you can make something up.

WRITING TIP

Don't assume the reader knows what job you are interested in! Be sure to include an introduction.

Editing and Rewriting

Editing Present Unreal Conditional Sentences

In Chapter 10, page 124, you studied information about *real* conditional sentences. This section presents information about *un*real present conditionals.

1. *Study these rules.*

> **Unreal** conditional sentences explain what *would happen* under a certain condition.

Rules	*Examples*
a. In the *if*-clause in a present unreal condition, use the past form of the verb to show that the condition is not true.	If I **had** a different job, . . . If we **worked** in the cafeteria, . . .
b. Use **were** (not **was**) in the *if*-clause in a present unreal condition.	If I **were** you, . . . If she **were** the president, . . . If I **were able to have** any job in the world, . . .
c. When the *if*-clause begins the sentence, it is separated from the rest of the sentence by a comma (,).	If you **didn't go** to work every day,⤶.
d. Use **would** in the result clause to show that it is not true. You can also use **could** or **might,** depending on the meaning. These modals are always followed by the simple form of the verb.	If I were you, I **would talk** to your boss. If he understood the problem, he **would do** something about it. If he understood the problem, he **could help** us. If she were here, she **might know** the answer.
e. In many cases, the condition is stated only once and the result idea continues through many sentences.	If I didn't have to work, I **would** probably **do** volunteer work. I **would try** to work in education, because I like to work with young people. I **wouldn't want** to stay home.

2. *Put a check (✓) in front of the sentence(s) with correct verb forms.*

a. _____ If I work in a factory, I would probably make a good salary.

b. _____ If he didn't have a job, he wouldn't be able to pay his rent.

c. _____ If you don't have to work, would you?

d. _____ If they couldn't find a job, they might move.

(ANSWER KEY)

3. *Correct any mistakes in verbs in these sentences. Not every sentence has a mistake.*

(a) If I were a doctor, I work with children. (b) I wouldn't wanted to be a surgeon. (c) A surgeon wouldn't get to know the patients very well.

(d) If I get this job, I worked hard to contribute to your company. (e) I have always wanted to work in construction, so I would consider this a great opportunity.

(f) I don't have any experience in this area, but I would work harder because of this. (g) I appreciate having the opportunity to talk with you about my experience in an interview.

Editing Checklist

Check the Content

1. *Exchange your self-evaluation with a classmate. After you read what your classmate wrote, answer the question.*

   ❑ Is the self-evaluation complete and easy to read? Underline expressions or sentences that are not clear.

Check the Details

2. *Now, reread your self-evaluation. If necessary, revise what you wrote. Rewrite any unclear words or sentences. Add more details if necessary. Then continue checking your own writing. Use these questions.*

   ❑ Did you use transition words to show contrast? Check the punctuation with these words.
   ❑ Check each verb. Did you use the correct tense?

3. *Make your corrections and rewrite your self-evaluation.*

Vocabulary Log

What words or phrases would you like to remember from this chapter? Write five to ten items in your notebook. Examples are on page 11.

Grammar and Punctuation Review

Look over your writing from this chapter. What changes did you need to make in grammar and punctuation? Write them in your notebook. Review all the grammar and punctuation problems you recorded in your notebook. Make a list of the ones that you still need to work on.

Reference

BUSINESS LETTER FORMAT

The format of a business letter is more formal than a personal letter.
This example is the **full block style.** All the lines of text are lined up on the left.

First and last name *Street address* *City, Country*	Carl Brodschi 414 River Road Louisville, KY 40207
Date	March 20, 1998
Name and address of person you are writing to	Suzanne Grant Director, Housing Office Boston University 66 Bay State Road Boston, MA 02215
Salutation	Dear Ms. Grant:
Text of the letter	I will be attending Boston University next year. Please send me information about student housing and an application form.
Closing statement	Thank you very much.
Closing phrase	Sincerely,
Signature	*Carl Brodschi*
Printed name	Carl Brodschi

This is the **modified block style.** The first line of each paragraph may be indented three spaces.

Sender's name and address	Carl Brodschi 414 River Road Louisville, KY 40207
Date	March 20, 1998
Name and address of person you are writing to	Suzanne Grant Director, Housing Office Boston University 66 Bay State Road Boston, MA 02215
Salutation	Dear Ms. Grant:
Text of the letter	I will be attending Boston University next year. Please send me information about student housing and an application form.
Closing statement	Thank you very much.
Closing phrase	Sincerely,
Signature	*Carl Brodschi*
Printed name	Carl Brodschi

COMPARATIVES AND SUPERLATIVES

Use these rules to form the comparative and superlative forms of adjectives, adverbs, and nouns.

Rule	Comparative	Superlative	Example
one-syllable adjective or adverb	-er . . . than	the . . . -est	**faster** than (fast) the **hardest** (hard)
two-syllable adjective or adverb ending in **-y**; change the **y** to **i**	-ier . . . than	the . . . -iest	**easier** than (easy) the **busiest** (busy)
adjective or adverb of two (or more) syllables	more . . . than	the most . . .	more **exciting** the most **enthusiastic**
count noun	more . . . than fewer . . . than	the most . . . the fewest . . .	more **jobs** than the most **jobs** fewer **rewards** than the fewest **rewards**
noncount noun	more . . . than less . . . than	the most . . . the least . . .	more **discipline** than the most **discipline** less **money** than the least **money**
irregular forms	good well bad badly far	better better worse worse farther	the best the best the worst the worst the farthest

Holidays

Malaysia

Wesak is an important Buddhist holiday in Malaysia. This is a day in spring to remember important events in Buddha's life, such as his birth and his death. All of the temples in the country are full of people who burn incense, pray, and give food to the poor. The monks in their saffron-colored robes chant prayers. There is also a candle procession. For me, the most beautiful moment is when doves are set free.

Kuwait

There are different *Eid's* in my country, but my favorite is the *Eid Al-Adha,* the "Feast of Sacrifice." We always sacrifice a sheep on this day. I don't know what the date is on a Western calendar, but it is the tenth day of the twelfth Islamic month. We go to the mosque to pray and then spend time with our families. This feast marks the end of the pilgrimage to Mecca.

United States

When I was a child, Halloween was my favorite holiday. It is always on October 31. Children dress up in costumes, especially scary ones, and go door to door, saying "Trick or treat!" They get candy from each house. People carve faces out of pumpkins, put candles in them, and place them outside their homes. This is a very old custom, and the original purpose was to scare away evil spirits.

Japan

March 3 is my favorite holiday in Japan, *Hina-masturi,* the "Doll Festival." This is a holiday to wish for the future happiness of girls. We set up *Hina* dolls in traditional kimonos on a stair display and have friends over for a party. We also have special traditional food. After this day, it's very important to put the dolls away as soon as possible or we won't ever get married!

Russia

When I lived in Russia, I never knew Jewish holidays, but after I immigrated to Israel, I began to celebrate them. *Purim* is the one I like the best. The day varies, depending on the Jewish calendar, but it is always in the spring. On this day we commemorate an important victory over evil in ancient Jewish history. There are carnivals, singing, and shaking of noisy toys in the street. It is a very joyful holiday, and children exchange baskets of toys and candy, and postcards with funny wishes.

China

My favorite Chinese holiday is the Dragon Boat Festival. It falls on the fifth day of the fifth moon on the Chinese calendar. We eat a pyramid-shaped mass of glutinous rice wrapped in leaves on this day and hang up a string of leaves outside our homes to scare away goblins. There is a reenactment of the story of this holiday: a famous poet's suicide when he was publicly shamed by a king. Ancient people believed the poet didn't die but continued to live under the water. That's why we eat the rice wrapped in leaves. Leaves don't get wet, and they protect the rice for the poet.

Korea

May is Gratitude Month in Korea, and May 15 is Teachers' Day. We have a lot of respect for teachers, so we give them red carnations on this day. A carnation means "thanks" in flower language. There are special functions at schools, and we send thank-you cards to our former teachers.

IRREGULAR SIMPLE PAST TENSE VERBS

Base	Simple Past	Past Participle	Base	Simple Past	Past Participle
awake	awoke	awoken	leave	left	left
bear	born	born	lend	lend	lend
beat	beat	beaten	let	let	let
became	become	become	lie	lay	lain
begin	began	begun	light	lit/lighted	lit/lighted
bend	bent	bent	lost	lost	lost
bet	bet	bet	make	made	made
bid	bid	bid	mean	meant	meant
bite	bit	bitten	make	made	made
bleed	bled	bled	meet	met	met
blow	blew	blown	put	put	put
break	broke	broken	prove	proved	proven
bring	brought	brought	quit	quit	quit
build	built	built	read	read	read
burn	burnt/burned	burnt/burned	rid	rid	rid
burst	burst	burst	ride	rode	ridden
buy	bought	bought	ring	rang	rung
cast	cast	cast	rise	rose	risen
catch	caught	caught	run	ran	run
choose	chose	chosen	say	said	said
come	came	come	see	saw	seen
cost	cost	cost	seek	sought	sought
creep	crept	crept	sell	sold	sold
cut	cut	cut	send	sent	sent
deal	dealt	dealt	set	set	set
dig	dug	dug	shake	shook	shaken
dive	dove	dived	shine	shone	shone
	(British: dived)		shoot	shot	shot
do	did	done	shrink	shrank	shrunk
draw	drew	drawn	shut	shut	shut
dream	dreamt/	dreamt/	sing	sang	sung
	dreamed	dreamed	sink	sank	sunk
drink	drank	drunk	sit	sat	sat
drive	drove	driven	sleep	slept	slept
eat	ate	eaten	slide	slid	slid
fall	fell	fallen	slit	slit	slit
feed	fed	fed	speak	sloke	spoken
feel	felt	felt	spend	spent	spent
fight	fought	fought	spin	spun	spun
find	found	found	split	split	split
fit	fit	fit	spread	spread	spread
fly	flew	flown	spring	sprang	sprung
forbid	forbid/forbade	forbidden	stand	stood	stood
forget	forgot	forgotten	steal	stole	stolen
forgive	forgave	forgiven	stick	stuck	stuck
freeze	froze	frozen	sting	stung	stung
get	got	gotten	strike	struck	struck
		(British: got)	swear	swore	sworn
give	gave	given	sweep	swept	swept
go	went	gone	swim	swam	swum
grind	ground	ground	swing	swung	swung
grow	grew	grown	take	took	taken
hang	hung	hung	teach	taught	taught
have	had	had	tear	tore	torn
hear	heard	heard	tell	told	told
hide	hid	hidden/hid	think	thought	thought
hit	hit	hit	throw	threw	thrown
hold	held	held	wake	woke	woken
hurt	hurt	hurt	wear	wore	worn
keep	kept	kept	wet	wet	wet
knit	knit	knitted	win	won	won
know	knew	known	withdraw	withdrew	withdrawn
lay	laid	laid	wind	wound	wound or winded
lead	led	led			

NONCOUNT NOUNS

Some nouns do not have a plural form because we cannot count them. We call these *noncount* nouns. Follow these rules when you use a noncount noun:

Rules	Examples
Noncount nouns are singular. If they are the subject of the sentence, the verb must be singular too.	The **milk is** on the table. His **news is** not good. The **homework was** easy.
Do not use *a* or *an* with a noncount noun.	We need **milk.**
Use a quantity expression to make a noncount noun countable.	Please get **a gallon of milk.** I have **lots of homework** tonight.

Here are some common noncount nouns:

Groups of similar items	art, clothing, equipment, food, fruit, furniture, garbage, grammar, homework, information, luggage, mail, money, music, news, research, slang, traffic, vocabulary, work
Liquids	beer, blood, coffee, cream, gasoline, honey, juice, milk, oil, shampoo, soda, soup, tea, water, wine
Things that can be cut into smaller pieces	bread, butter, cheese, cotton, film, glass, gold, ice, iron, meat, paper, silver, wood
Things that have very small parts	dirt, flour, grass, hair, rice, sand, sugar
Gases	air, fog, pollution, smog, smoke, steam
Ideas that you cannot touch	advice, anger, beauty, communication, education, fun, happiness, health, help, love, luck, peace, sleep, space, time, truth, wealth
Fields of study	business administration, engineering, nursing
Activities	soccer, swimming, tennis, traveling
Diseases and illnesses	cancer, cholera, flu, heart disease, malaria, polio, smallpox, strep throat
Facts or events of nature	darkness, electricity, fire, fog, heat, light, lightning, rain, snow, sunshine, thunder, weather, wind
Languages	Arabic, Chinese, Turkish, Russian

SPELLING RULES FOR ADDING ENDINGS

To apply spelling rules, remember that the vowels in English are **a, e, i, o,** and **u.** The rest of the letters are consonants. When you add endings to nouns or verbs, follow these rules:

Plural Noun Endings

For most nouns	add **-s.**	book	books
For nouns that end in **s, x, ch,** or **sh**	add **-es.**	box	boxes
		wish	wishes
For nouns that end in **z**	double the **z** and add **-es.**	quiz	quizzes
For nouns that end in a consonant + **y**	change the **y** to **i** and add **-es.**	delivery	deliveries

Verb Endings

For verbs that end in a consonant + **e**	drop the **-e** and add **-ing** or **-ed.**	hope	hoping	hoped
For one-syllable verbs that end in one vowel + a consonant	double the consonant and add **-ing** or **-ed.**	stop	stopping	stopped
For two-syllable verbs that have the stress on the second syllable and end in a vowel + a consonant	double the consonant and add **-ing** or **-ed.**	omit	omitting	omitted
For verbs that end in a consonant + **y**	change the **y** to **i** and add **-ed** or **-es.**	try	tried	tries
For verbs that end in **o, (t)ch, s, sh, x,** or **z**	add **-es.**	do	does	
		match	matches	
		toss	tosses	
		wish	wishes	
		fix	fixes	
		buzz	buzzes	

TRANSITION EXPRESSIONS

When you combine sentences or ideas, transition expressions help make your ideas clear.

Start with two separate ideas or sentences.	I ate breakfast. I went to the store at 10:00 a.m.
Combine the ideas with a **preposition**.	I went to the store **after** breakfast.
Combine the ideas with a **subordinate conjunction**.	I went to the store **after** I ate breakfast. I ate breakfast **before** I went to the store.
Combine the ideas with an **adverbial expression**.	I ate breakfast. **After that,** I went to the store. I went to the store. **Before that,** I ate breakfast.

Here are some common transition expressions.

Prepositions	Subordinate Conjunctions	Adverbial Expressions
Time in a Sequence		
after, before, until	after, before, until (till)	at this point, before that, in the past, (not) long ago, after that, at first, in the future
• We waited **until** 3:15.	• We waited **until** they came.	• We weren't angry **at first** • **At first,** we weren't angry.
Listing		
		first, in the first place, in the second place, later on, then, after that, next, finally, last
		• **First,** try to write down the problem. **Then** telephone the landlord.
At the Same Time		
during	when, as, while, as long as	meanwhile, at the same time, at that time
• They watch TV **during** dinner.	• They watch TV **when** they eat dinner.	• I waited in line at the ticket counter. **Meanwhile,** my father returned the rental car.

Prepositions	Subordinate Conjunctions	Adverbial Expressions
Contrast		
unlike, in contrast to	but	however, in contrast, on the other hand,
• **Unlike** my sister, I like cold weather.	• I like cold weather, **but** my sister doesn't.	• I like cold weather. My sister, **on the other hand,** hates it.
Cause-Effect, Results, Reasons		
because of, as a result of	because, since, so, as	for this reason, because of this, as a result, therefore, so
• She was unhappy **because of** her living situation.	• She was unhappy **because** she didn't like her roommates. • Her roommates never talked to her, **so** she didn't feel comfortable in her apartment.	• Her roommates almost never spoke. **Because of this,** she was very unhappy in her apartment.
Condition		
	if, unless	
	• **If** it rains, we won't go to the beach. • We'll go to the beach **unless** it rains.	
Examples		
such as		for example
• I like sports **such as** ice-skating that keep you warm in the winter.		• Some winter sports are better than others. **For example,** ice-skating keeps you warm and is great exercise.

Answer Key

I New Directions

CHAPTER 1

Reading (*pages 3–5*)

2. (*page 4*)
a. talk to your teacher; b. no; c. more student-centered;
d. because of review days; e. no; f. usually guide and give
opportunities for practice and feedback; don't lecture.
3. (*pages 4–5*)
a. lectures; b. named, called; c. apologized, explained;
d. opportunities, practice, practice; e. feedback; f. ask,
interrupt; g. reviewed, practice
4. (*page 5*)
a. go over; b. make sure; c. basics

Editing for Verb Forms (*pages 8–9*)

2. (*page 9*)
a, d, e, f
3. (*page 9*)
b. <u>bus</u>, leaves; c. <u>He</u>, must pay; d. are; <u>places</u>; e. <u>One</u>, is;
f. <u>You</u>, should try; g. <u>bus ride</u>, takes; h. are, <u>a lot of ethnic
restaurants</u>, i. is, <u>place</u>; j. <u>You</u>, should try; k. <u>office supply
store</u>, has; l. <u>drugstore</u>, sells

CHAPTER 2

Reading (*pages 14–17*)

2. (*page 15*)
b. state, <u>in the state of</u>; c. no, <u>originally French</u>; d. Vieux
Carré, <u>also known as</u>; e. a type of pastry, <u>a type of pastry</u>;
f. of the world, <u>means 'of the world'</u>; g. a lovely park, <u>a
lovely park</u>; h. a historical museum, <u>a historical museum</u>;
i. the oldest apartment buildings in the United States, <u>the
oldest apartment buildings in the United States</u>
4. (*page 17*)
musician, artist, tourist, historical, beautiful

Reflect on Reading (*page 16*)

1. Italics; 2. parentheses, a comma; 3. Quotation marks

Targeting: Frequently Confused Words (*pages 17–20*)

2. (*pages 19–20*)
b. Others; c. most of; d. Most; e. Another; f. Most;
g. Most of; h. Almost; i. The other; j. Another; k. almost

CHAPTER 3

Reading 1 (*pages 24–26*)

1. (*pages 24–25*)
a. They go in opposite directions.; b. the places where the
bus stops; c. well-known places (listed in the legend on
the right)
2. (*pages 25–26*)
a. a.m.; b. bus stops; c. 13 minutes; d. 5:30 a.m.;
e. 6:45 a.m.

Reading 2 (*pages 27–29*)

2. (*page 27*)

	Jack	Peter	Sarah	Carla	Ingrid
takes the bus			✓		
rides a bicycle		✓			
walks	✓	✓	✓		✓
rides a boat or ferry	✓		✓		
drives			✓	✓	

3. (*page 27*)
Jack Loring: across the lake from the university
Peter Jefferson: near the university
Sarah Schmidt: on the island
Carla Thompson: south of the airport
Ingrid Sunstren: at the university
4. (*page 28*)
Jack: traffic on the bridge; Peter: rain, being hit by car;
Sarah: more than an hour and a half to get to work; Carla:
bus took too long, not near office, traffic; Ingrid: delayed
by cafeteria line, never leaves enough time
6. (*page 29*)
Vocabulary: traffic, commute, bridge across lake, boat,
walk, ride my bicycle, car, crossing the street, park my car,
passenger ferry, ferry ride, take the bus, arrive later.
Discussions will vary.

Reading 3 (*pages 29–31*)

1. (*page 29*)
3, 2, 1, 5, 4 (**Note:** The story describes this scene first, but
the sequence of events begins with the travel agency
scene described in paragraph 2)

2. (*page 30*)
Sequence: My first problem, The next day; *Contrast:*
Instead, However, but; *Cause or Result:* As a result, because
3. (*page 31*)
b. F; c. F; d. F; e. F; f. T
4. (*page 31*)
Answers may vary; b. important, check; c. hard, believe;
d. important, keep; e. impossible, remember; f. fun, tell

Editing for Present and Past Tense (*pages 33–35*)

2. (*page 33*)
will never forget, am, could order, I'm going, can . . .
imagine
3. (*page 34*)
a. has; b. had; c. has; d. has to; e. takes; f. is; g. gets; h. falls;

i. got; j. fell; k. woke; l. stopped; m. had; n. was; o. was;
p. were; q. had to; r. turned out

2 The Language of Gestures

CHAPTER 4

Starting Point (*pages 38–40*)

2. (*pages 38–40*)
b. hug; c. bow; d. pat, back; e. shake hands, someone's;
f. smile, eye contact

Reading 1 (*pages 40–45*)

2. (*page 41*)
a. 2; b. 3; c. 1
3. (*pages 41–42*)
a. 3; b. 2; c. 1
4. (*page 42*)
b. face; c. hand; d. feelings; e. facial gestures;
f. body language
5. (*page 43*)
a. 3; b. 4; c. 2
6. (*pages 43–44*)
a. 2; b. 2; c. 3; d. 1; e. 3
7. (*page 45*)
b. 4; c. 6; d. 7; e. 1; f. 2; g. 3
8. (*page 45*)
b. the black part of the eye; c. how you dress and how you
hold yourself; d. how you hold yourself; e. figure out

Reading 2 (*pages 46–49*)

2. (*page 47*)
b. F; c. T; d. F; e. F; f. F; g. F; h. T; i. F ; j. T; k. T
5. (*page 48*)
a. routinely, really, automatically, sincerely, deeply b. -*ly*
6. (*page 48*)
a. usually; b. usual; c. lightly; d. light; e. sincere;
f. sincerely; g. automatic; h. automatically; i. routine;
j. routinely
7. (*page 49*)
a.

Noun	*Verb*	*Adjective*
greeting	greet	———
extension	*extend*	extended
connection	*connect*	connected
knowledge	know	*knowledgeable*
interest	interest	*interesting*
respect	*respect*	respectful
		respected
appreciation	*appreciate*	appreciated

b. -*ion*
c. -*ful, -ed*

Targeting: Transitions (*pages 49–51*)

2. (*page 50*)
Paragraph 1: *also*—hand gestures
The third way—body movement
Paragraph 2: *also*—warmth
finally—negative feelings
3. (*page 51*)
Second; also; third type of

Preparing to Write: Organizing Information (*pages 51–53*)

3. (*page 53*)
b, d
4. (*page 53*)
a. When you meet an older male relative, you bow to him.
The older male will probably pat you on the back or shake
hands with you.
c. The *wai* is the most common greeting in Thailand. To
make the *wai,* first put the (your) hands together in front
of the (your) chest and bow the (your) head slightly.

CHAPTER 5

Targeting: Ways to Give Instructions (*pages 60–61*)

2. (*page 61*)
your, should, be, Keep, your, Keep, you, your

Preparing to Write: Information in Instructions (*pages 61–62*)

2. (*page 61*)
hand, head, face, palm, hand, wrist, forearm, hand (8) first;
Next, Finally

CHAPTER 6

Reading (*pages 65–69*)

2. (*pages 67–68*)
a. The United States; Asian countries
b. *Touch Countries*: Middle Eastern Countries (*given*), Latin
American countries, Italy, Greece, Spain, Portugal, some
Asian countries, Russia (*Middle column*): France, China,
Ireland (*given*), India *Nontouch countries*: United States,
Japan, Canada, England, Scandinavia, northern European
countries, Australia, Estonia
3. (*page 69*)
a. T; b. T; c. F; d. F; e. T; f. T

Editing for Consistent Formatting (*pages 73–74*)

2. (*page 74*)
b
3. (*page 74*)

Number of People	2	4
Position in Elevator	two back corners	all four corners

3 Pets or Pests?

CHAPTER 7

Reading (*pages 78–80*)

2. (*pages 79*)
b, c, a
3. (*page 80*)
a. F; b. F; c. T; d. F; e. F; f. T; g. T; h. T
4. (*page 80*)
humorous, colorful, moody, intelligent, musical, international, capable of feelings

Targeting: Adjectives (*pages 80–81*)

1. colorful; 2. color; 3. humor; 4. humorous; 5. mood;
6. moody; 7. talkative; 8. talk; 9. musical; 10. music, music;
11. romantic; 12. romance; 13. impression;
14. impressionable

Preparing to Write: Providing Supporting Ideas (*pages 82–84*)

2. (*pages 83–84*)
b. 2, A random survey of ESL students in our program regarding their pet preferences showed that dogs are the most popular pet.; c. 3,1, Cats are more interesting than dogs.; d. 1, My dog Salsaree was a very fierce dog.; e. 2, I think Americans try to extend their pets' lives too long with expensive medical treatments.; f. 1, Dogs are very intelligent.; g. 2,3, According to the documentary *Our Feathered Friends,* without love and companionship, parrots will become mentally ill, and no amount of love can cure them.

Editing for Sentence Completeness (*pages 84–86*)

2. (*pages 85–86*)
a. they are; b. but; c. ~~who~~; d. are; e. We don't have a pet because . . . . *or* Because we aren't home enough to take care of a pet, we don't have any pets.; f. am; g. We didn't have pets because, in my house, my mother was always worried about cleanliness. *or* Because in my house my mother was always worried about cleanliness, we didn't have pets.; h. they will; i. If you don't talk to your bird, it will be lonely.; j. was

CHAPTER 8

Reading (*pages 89–94*)

2. (*page 90*)
b. *Some answers may vary. Possible answers follow*: Pets (Dogs and cats) *or* Having dogs and cats (pets); c. Pets; d. you may make new friends.; e. When people talk to pets,; f. they want to get well.; g. they began to smile and cooperate with the doctors.
3. (*page 91*)
Answers may vary slightly. Possible answers follow: Physical

Health: Pets help you exercise.; help keep blood pressure low.
Mental Health: You don't feel lonely.; Pets provide love, companionship, and affection.; Pets help you make more friends.; They make you laugh, lift your spirits, take your mind off your troubles.; Pets give you a sense of self-worth.
4. (*pages 91–92*)
a. 4; b. 5; c. 1 or 2; d. 6; e. 7; f. 8; g. 3; h. 2
5. (*page 93*)
discover, convenient, satisfy, researcher, loneliness, affection, international, depressed, cooperate, development
6. (*pages 93–94*)
a. -ment; b. -ers; c. -ed; d. -al; e. -y; f. -t; g. -ion;
h. -liness; i. -ed; j. -e

Preparing to Write: Adding Specific Details (*pages 94–99*)

5. (*page 97*)
c, a, d, b
6. (*pages 97–98*)
a. I would like my turtle to be in your program.
b. My cat would be very good in your visiting pet program.
c. I would very much like my German shepherd to be in your program.
d. I am writing to tell you about my very affectionate pet guinea pig.

Editing for Errors in Present Perfect Tense (*pages 100–102*)

2. (*page 102*)
a. (correct); b. (*given*) c. ~~has~~ opened; d. (correct);
e. ~~were~~ have been; f. ~~was~~ has been; g. (correct); h. ~~has~~ knocked; i. (correct); j. ~~has known~~ knows; k. ~~has come~~ comes

CHAPTER 9

Reading (*pages 104–106*)

2. (*page 105*)
Animals and complaints: a. a (small) dog—makes a mess in the garden (*or* grass); b. cats—have fleas, come into apartment; c. parrot—squawks all day; d. guinea pigs—smell bad; e. snake—creepy, in the laundry room (basket);
f. cat—allergic to cats; g. dog—barks at night
4. (*page 106*)
a. I can't take it anymore. b. I am sick and tired of . . .
c. . . . is driving me crazy; I can't stand . . .
d. This is just too much; The . . . is terrible.
e. But I don't like to. . . . It's creepy. It's making me nuts.
f. It's a nightmare.
g. The . . . is too much.
5. (*page 106*)
a. patio, balcony; b. Fleas; c. Guinea pigs; d. exotic;
e. coiled; f. allergic

Editing for Errors with Singular Count Nouns (*pages 111–112*)

2. (*page 112*)
a. (*given*); b. <u>animals</u>, <u>reactions</u>, <u>people</u>; c. <u>haters</u>,
d. a serious cat <u>hater</u>; e. <u>people</u>, <u>cats</u>, the (his) <u>property</u>;
f. <u>lovers</u>, the Islamic <u>prophet</u>; g. <u>cat</u>, the sleeve of his robe;
h. <u>prayers</u>, the <u>cat</u>; i. the <u>sleeve</u> of his (the) <u>robe</u>; j. (*correct*),
<u>lover</u>; k. his <u>cat</u>; l. <u>meetings</u>, the <u>war</u>; m. a (the) Nobel
Peace Prize <u>winner</u>, left <u>hands</u>, his <u>cat</u>, n. his left <u>hand</u>;
o. his left <u>arm</u>, his right <u>hand</u>

4 Healthy Choices

CHAPTER 10

Reading 1 (*pages 116–120*)

2. (*page 118*)
a. also; b. "even though <u>walking is so natural</u>" refers to
"<u>we were designed to walk</u>"; c. adds
3. (*page 118*)
a. 3; b. 2; c. 5; d. 1; e. 4
5. (*page 119*)
(*References are to list in box "Tips for Buying Walking
Shoes."*) b. bullet 7; c. bullet 5; d. bullet 2; e. bullet 1;
f. bullet 3
6. (*page 119*)
a. adjust, lessen; b. depression, anxiety; c. improve,
increased; d. significantly, gradually; e. strolled, walked

Reading 2 (*pages 120–122*)

2. (*page 121*)
a. 7; b. 4; c. 5; d. 1; e. 6; f. 3; g. 2
3. (*pages 121–122*)
a. F; b. T; c. T; d. F; e. F; f. F

Preparing to Write: Organizing Information (*pages 122–123*)

5. (*page 123*)
outline 2

Editing Real Conditional Sentences (*pages 124–125*)

2. (*page 125*)
a. ~~will~~ walk; b. get; c. walk~~ed~~; d. ~~will~~ walk; e. walk~~ed~~
3. (*page 125*)
b. walk, will get; c. wear, won't get (become); d. change,
won't get (become); e. walk, will be; f. will be, take

CHAPTER 11

Reading (*pages 128–130*)

2. (*page 129*)
(*Wording of answers may vary.*)
a. control your weight
b. [first line] fatty deposits form; [second line] blood
   doesn't flow well

c. help the body get rid of cholesterol
3. (*page 129*)
a. baked chicken; b. fish; c. vegetables; d. sunflower oil
4. (*pages 129–130*)
Across: 1. diet; 4. rid; 5. fat; 7. dietary; 8. deposits;
11. arteriosclerosis
Down: 2. intake; 3. trim; 5. food; 6. arteries; 9. produce;
10. weight; 12. limit; 13. reduce

Editing for Noncount Nouns (*pages 132–135*)

2. (*page 134*)
(*Only noncount nouns are indicated.*)
a. rice, dinner; d. milk; e. olive oil, butter; f. lunch;
g. sugar, vinegar; h. information; i. cholesterol
4. (*page 135*)
b. (*no change*); c. (*no change*); d. much fat; e. (*no change*);
f. (*no change*); g. (*no change*); h. (*no change*); i. meat; j. (*no
change*); k. more international food or many international
foods; l. ~~A~~ Good food; m. (*no change*); n. more energy;
o. Lunchtime; p. (*no change*); q. (*no change*); r. Good music,
tablecloths, fresh flowers; s. ~~a~~ colorful food; t. time; u. (*no
change*); v. healthy take-home dinners; w. (*no change*);
x. grocery shopping

CHAPTER 12

Reading 1 (*pages 138–141*)

2. (*page 139*)
3, 1, 2
3. (*page 139*)
a. 1; b. 3; c. 2
4. (*page 139*)
a. 3; b. 4; c. 2; d. 1
5. (*page 140*)

	(*given*)	(*given*)	(*Answers may vary.*)
eco-	*environment*	ecopsychology	*ecology*
en-	*in*	environment	*envelope*
co-	*together, with*	connected	*convention*
dis-	*not*	disconnected	*dislike*
over-	*beyond what is necessary*	overdeveloping	*oversleep*
ir-	*not*	irresponsible	*irregular*
re-	*again*	reconnect	*review*

6. (*page 141*)

	Example from Reading	Another Example (*Answers may vary.*)
psych:	psychology	psychological
velop:	overdevelop	envelope
struct:	destructive	structure
nat:	nature	native

Reflect on Reading (*page 140*)

a

Reading 2 (*pages 141–143*)

2. (*page 143*)
a. We need to stop rushing.
b. rushing
c. paying attention
d. We do things wrong and spend more time in the end. We have no time to talk to people, so we get lonelier. We don't notice important signs that something is wrong. We consume more than we need.
e. (*Answers may vary.*) *Possible answer:* Pay attention to your speed and consciously slow down.
f. looking at everything in your life and appreciating it
g. Our lifestyle causes discontent and resentment because we always want more.
h. to remember what is important in life
i. *Possible answers follow:* the rules for capitalization (in the poet's name and in the poem), the rules for punctuation, word order ("amazing most day" instead of "most amazing day"), invented words ("leaping greenly spirits of trees")

Targeting: Collocations (*pages 144–145*)

3. (*page 145*)
b. climbing; c. ~~to~~ destroying; d. ~~to~~; e. (*correct*);
f. ~~to~~ looking

Preparing to Write: Analyzing Information (*pages 145–149*)

3. (*pages 147–149*)

	a	b	c	d
analyzes an individual's lifestyle	✓		✓	✓
analyzes a group's lifestyle		✓	✓	
describes the present		✓	✓	✓
describes the past	✓		✓	✓
describes the pace of life	✓	✓	✓	
describes the relationship to nature		✓		✓

5 Celebrate!

CHAPTER 13

Starting Point (*pages 153–155*)

1. (*pages 153–154*)
a. 2; b. 4; c. 1; d. 3

Reading (*pages 155–157*)

1. (*page 155*)
a. 3; b. 2; c. 1
2. (*pages 156–157*)
a. 2; b. 4; c. 1

3. (*page 157*)
a. 3; b. 4; c. 1; d. 2

Editing for Article and Noun Errors in Generalizations (*pages 160–161*)

2. (*page 161*)
a. (*correct*); b. traditions; c. customs; d. countries;
e. (*correct*); f. generations; g. A second, grapes; h. months;
i. grapes, the table; j. a trip, a packed suitcase (*or* packed suitcases); k. an (*or* the) old calendar(s); l. calendars

CHAPTER 14

Starting Point (*page 163*)

1. (*page 163*)
a. Keep America Beautiful Month; e. Secretaries' Week;
b. Library Forgiveness Week; c. International Guitar Month

Reading (*pages 163–165*)

2. (*page 165*)
b. Take Your Daughter to Work Day; c. girls; d. Take Your Daughter to Work Day; e. mothers, fathers, or other adults; f. a female road worker g. Take Your Daughter to Work Day; h. Some people think this day is not fair to boys.; i. Keep Our Sons at Home Day
3. (*pages 165*)
b. F; c. T; d. T

Preparing to Write: Steps for Writing a Summary (*pages 167–168*)

1. (*page 167*)
b. six million girls, participate, Take Your Daughter to Work Day
c. April, 9- to 14-year-old girls watch women, working outside home
d. Take Your Daughter to Work Day began 1990s, important, girls feel they can succeed, workplace
e. Not everyone, happy, some don't like, children at work, others, not fair to boys
f. some companies, Take Your Child to Work Day, other people, suggested, Keep Our Sons at Home Day, boys, learn about, homemaking and rearing children
2. (*pages 167–168*)
a. 2; b. 1; c. 2; d. 3; e. 2; f. 2

CHAPTER 15

Reading 1 (*pages 171–173*)

1. (*page 171*)
a. Southern California (Los Angeles); b. the Garlic Festival;
c. the Garlic Festival; d. JW Events: Dennis Yeomans;
e. free ; f. Taste of Kosher L.A.; g. Taste of Orange County
2. (*page 172*)
a. Seattle, Washington; b. more than 6,000 participants from over 100 countries, 18 stages, 1,000 performances, and an audience of nearly 200,000; c. Memorial Day weekend

3. (*page 173*)
a. a folklife festival; b. nearly 200,000; c. 1972; d. it's free;
e. 1. festival dates and times, 2. getting to the festival,
3. general program information, 4. how to participate

Reading 2 (*pages 173–174*)

2. d. Ferguson's Hardware Store
e. tellers at First National Freestone Bank
a. (*given*) b. Fast Copy Center c. Mayor Bingham

Preparing to Write 2: Formal Thank You Expressions (*page 176*)

b. large litter bags; c. took a pie (pies) in the face,
challenge; d. the kickoff breakfast for the community;
e. free photocopying of the flyer

Editing for Appropriate Language in Formal Letters (*page 177*)

a. 2; b. 1; c. 2; d. 1

6 Getting Down to Work

CHAPTER 16

Reading (*pages 181–183*)

2. (*page 182*)
a. 4; b. 2; c. 5; d. 1 (*given*); e. 3
3. (*page 182*)
a. F; b. T; c. F; d. T; e. F; f. F; g. T
4. (*page 182*)
c
5. (*page 183*)
b. housing; c. ability; d. make a difference; e. volunteer;
f. trails; g. poll; h. coach; i. unlimited

Editing for Word Forms: Adjectives and Adverbs (*pages 185–186*)

2. (*pages 185–186*)
b. free; c. eagerly; d. immediately; e. voluntarily;
f. happy
3. (*page 186*)
b, d, e

CHAPTER 17

Reading 1 (*pages 189–190*)

2. (*page 190*)
a. (reading down columns): executive secretary; research
technician; cruise ship restaurant workers; construction
laborer; entry level account executive; construction
laborer (mailing machine operator) b. research technician;
entry level account executive c. executive secretary
d. answers will vary

Reading 2 (*pages 191–193*)

2. (*pages 191–192*)
a. breadwinners; b. volunteer (work); c. recent; d. afford;
e. options; f. complicated; g. responsibilities
3. (*page 192*)
a. 1; b. 2; c. 2; d. 1; e. 1
4. (*page 193*)

Women	Men
31%	21%
15%	33%
33%	28%
20%	17%

Targeting: Expressions for Reporting Results (*pages 193–194*)

1. (*page 193*)
b. were asked; c. percent of; d. of women, from, to, in,
survey
2. (*page 194*)
a. 4; b. 8; c. 6; d. 1; e. 2; f. 7; g. 3; h. 10; i. 9; j. 5

Editing for Verbs Tenses in a Report (*pages 196–197*)

2. (*page 197*)
a, c, e
3. (*page 197*)
a. would do; b. (*correct*); c. wanted; d. wanted; e. preferred;
f. chose; g. would do; h. preferred; i. (*correct*); j. wanted;
k. found; l. polled

CHAPTER 18

Reading (*pages 199–202*)

8. (*page 202*)
a. 2; b. true; c. 1; d. 3; e. 1
9. (*page 202*)
a. sold; b. owners; c. wages; d. production; e. boiler

Targeting: Transitions That Show Contrast (*pages 203–205*)

2. (*pages 203–204*)
(*Some answers may vary.*) b. but; c. On the one hand,
On the other hand; d. Compared to (with) e. However;
f. However; g. so; h. but, so; i. However

Editing for Present Unreal Conditional Sentences (*pages 206–208*)

2. (*pages 207–208*)
b, d
3. (*page 208*)
a. would work; b. wouldn't want; c. (*correct*);
d. would work; e. (*correct*); f. (*correct*); g. would
appreciate